Meditation
in the Yoga Tradition

The Practical Application to Begin,
or Enhance Your Meditation Practice

Nischala Joy Devi

Also, by Nischala Joy Devi

Books

The Healing Path of Yoga

The Secret Power of Yoga

The Namaste Effect

Online Courses

courses.abundantwellbeing.com

Audio

Abundant Wellbeing Series

Secret Power of Yoga

Namaste Effect

First edition - January 2020

To All Who Yearn

to Find the Light Within

Contents

Exploring Meditation

Meditation in the Yoga Tradition, encourages and offers inspiration, information and practices to anyone seeking to begin, sustain or enhance a meditation practice.

The yogic wisdom contained in this book augments the practices to inform the various way's meditation can be suited to every personality, mental or emotional perception.

Much of this wisdom comes from Scriptural Testimony, often quoted from the Secret Power of Yoga, a translation by Nischala Joy Devi of The Yoga Sutras of Patanjali.

The simple approach allows for assimilation of the varied techniques either in solitude or in tandem with other practices. They aid us in achieving a state of peace that comes from knowing the inner workings of the mind and emotions.

A strong commitment to regular practices is necessary for the state of meditation to be realized. The hope of this simple guide is to inspire your dedication to Knowing the Self, through meditation.

This awareness will lead to a Dynamic Stillness in everything you do and ultimately will reveal the light in your heart allowing you to know who you really are.

Enjoy reuniting with your inner light,

Om Shanthi

Chapter One

Meditation in the

Yoga Tradition

Meditation is that all pervasive feeling of peace which we experience as
a Dynamic Stillness. It is tool for total transformation.

As we begin the practice of meditation we delve into and slowly
understand its deep significance and place in our lives.

As a yearning for that peace and stillness blossoms the practice of
meditation has come to our everyday lives. The seed hidden deep
within had been planted long before. It is that, which links us with our
spiritual selves. We now need to take the time to nurture and water it.
With zest and dedication that seed grows allowing us to see the world
at many new levels, heights, depths.

Meditation helps us to acknowledge the essence of our being. Instead
of revolving around externals such as our bodies, minds, social and
professional life etc. we go deep to the very core. A place beyond all
thoughts and feelings. A stillness, a dynamic stillness when touched
blossoms and permeates all other aspects of our life. It favorably
transforms the way we see our bodies, thoughts, friends, and even the
world. The deeper in we go the more the outside seems to change.

Many scriptures attest to the plethora of spiritual benefits derived
from the practice of Meditation. The *Yoga Sutras of Patanjali,*
use the insights of these scriptures to depict the nature of
consciousness and the path to liberation. The *Yoga Sutras,* being
a great spiritual text and guide comprised of the 196 aphorisms,
were originally compiled and codified by the great sage Sri

Patanjali. It weaves together a beautiful tapestry of essential wisdom and insights that allow us to know our Divine nature.

Much of this wisdom contained in the Yoga Sutras has been distilled and simplified from earlier sacred texts: the *Vedas,* the *Upanishads,* the *Bhagavad-Gita,* and perhaps some Buddhist texts. *Meditation in the Yoga Tradition* will from time to time expound upon the *Yoga Sutras* as a way to show scriptural sanction for the methods and benefits of Meditation.

YOUR NATURE IS DIVINE

From the Yoga Sutras of Patanjali

1.2 Yoga is the uniting of consciousness in the heart.

Yoga, meaning "yoke" or "union," is described in second sutra of the *Yoga Sutras of Patanjali,* as *Yoga Chitta Vritti Nirodaha,* Yoga is the uniting of consciousness in the heart.

Deep within our hearts, we abide as pure Divine Consciousness. But with the material world pulling us every which way, our consciousness is drawn outward. As our knowledge of the Divine Self slowly fades, it takes with it the understanding of our true nature.

In trying to comprehend *Yoga Chitta Vritti Nirodaha,* look to the vibration of each word. *Chit* is pure universal consciousness and *chitta* is the same consciousness individually expressed. *Chit* is the ocean of consciousness, vast and unlimited. At birth each of us gathers a small quantity of this vastness and encases it in the temple of our heart, as *chitta,* individual consciousness. Held for many years, it remains unchanged. Then, at the end of our life, it is released back into the ocean of consciousness; the recognition of oneness causes the *chitta* to instantaneously re-unite with the *chit.*

Many translations of the Yoga Sutras link this sutra to notions of controlling one's mind, thoughts and emotions. They assert that Meditation is the way to achieve that. Trying to gather and control the multitude of thoughts and emotions with no knowledge of their origin is a daunting idea and a very difficult task.

It seems to be a compromised way of explaining the concept of consciousness to a culture that does not have roots in the belief that we are *all* Divine. It then reverts to a means of control which might work well in the world, but less so in the subtle realms.

The Scriptures seem to adhere to the belief that consciousness abides in the heart, rather than in the mind, as many believe. But when we realize that it is the *heart* that is the holder of our consciousness, reunion-once understood to be a difficult task-seems more likely.

When this sutra is translated referencing only the mind, the emphasis is on control, restraint, or some form of restriction. It encourages students to be harsh with the consciousness. But the heart responds more readily to tenderness and gentle, caring treatment of that consciousness. It is the best way to liberate it.

As consciousness unites, the mind, emotions and senses balance and become calm like a deep mountain lake, clear and still.

Imagine consciousness in all its purity as that clear mountain lake. Gazing into the lake, we can see the mirror image of the mountains that surround it. This pristine illumination mirrors our Divine nature. While all is still and calm, the heart rests in its Divine nature, as we experience love and oneness for all.

A gentle wind blows across the lake, and the clear images become slightly wavy. The crystal-clear reflection of the light is disturbed, yet the distorted image can still be seen. If the wind continues to strengthen, the reflection of the mountains is soon completely obliterated.

The wind represents our thoughts and emotions, at first gentle and then strengthening. As the wind increases, it stirs up the bottom of the lake, and the clarity of the reflection is replaced by muddy turbulence. It may happen occasionally at first, and then slowly without our realizing it, it becomes more and more frequent. Eventually, our Divine nature is no longer being luminously reflected.

After some time, this motion causes the shore to wash into the lake, forming sandbars. Our thoughts and feelings form these clusters of habitual patterns, tendencies, and potentialities called *Samskaras*. The *Samskaras* accrue by the constant churning of the thoughts and emotions. Whenever any thought or feeling encounters the wind it is easily fed into one of these patterns. Then our habits and tendencies

Finding us and seeing that in everyone

become set and the mountains, once reflected in the lake, disappear from view.

The pattern of habit, or *Samskara,* is difficult to change, as our consciousness is often unable to reconfigure the obvious. An unexpected change in circumstances can be missed if we look only for the predicted course. Once the sandbars have developed, it takes a great wind of change to modify their shape.

To achieve this state of peace and stillness, we practice steadying the mind, emotions and senses. This allows the heart to expand and for us to dwell in higher levels of consciousness.

When we understand the importance and are able to actualize this union, we find we are filled with Ananda (joy).

1.3 United in the heart, consciousness is steadied; then we abide in our true nature, joy.

When consciousness reunites and remains undisturbed, our true Divine nature is revealed as joy. The expression of this joy is infinite love, which encompasses and then transforms everything it touches. Everywhere we look, we see the reflection of our Divine and joyful nature.

Many of us have had a glimmer of this feeling when falling in love. Everything looks brighter; even gloomy days cannot dissuade us from our bliss. We radiate joy and greet the world with openness and clarity.

People smile at us, mirroring this loving energy back to us. This then serves to reminds us of who we truly are, and the glorious cycle continues.

It is important to understand how fragile this state can be. We are cautioned by Sutra 1.4

1.4 At other times, we identify with the rays of consciousness, which fluctuate and encourage our perceived suffering.

Identifying with murky thoughts and feelings is like looking in a distorted mirror or a muddied lake. Those images are often reinforced by the outside world. When we identify with grumpy or angry thoughts, the mind beams them outward. Similar thoughts and similar people are attracted to us as if magnetically. When we feel sad or fearful, friends who feel the same may call us. After all, misery loves company!

As we come to understand that our nature is joy and love, the perception of suffering is unable to take root. Realizing that we do not have to be bound by any one interpretation, we alter our mode of identification. We then recognize and relate to our highest consciousness.

Imagine yourself standing in front of an enormous structure, one so large that it does not appear to have any boundaries. It is adorned with many images, sayings and words, that keep you engrossed. Even if at times the writings and images are disturbing, you remain attentive.

Finally glancing around for a moment, you spot a small opening, not much larger than your eye. You never imagined this structure had any kind of depth. Its surface seemed so complete and all-encompassing.

Pressing your forehead to the wall, you peer through the small opening and are instantly transported to another reality, an incredibly beautiful scene filled with radiant light and glorious color. The disturbing images and messages that seemed so real only moments ago evaporate like rain touched by the sun's radiance as it emerges from the clouds. You are transported through the portal to a peaceful vision. Once you taste the joy of living in beauty and love, you no longer find anything captivating about suffering.

Only with this clarity is the state of Meditation possible.

A MEDITATIVE EXPERIENCE

Your True Nature as Love

Find a quiet place to either sit or lie comfortably.

Take in a few life-affirming breaths and let them out easily.

Gently bring the awareness to your heart center, the seat of consciousness.

Observe as the consciousness is drawn away from the heart, attracted by any discomfort in the body. It could be your leg or arm, or a cramp in the back or neck.

Gently gather the consciousness and draw it back to the heart.

Repeat silently or aloud, "Yoga is the uniting of consciousness in the heart, then I abide in my own true nature, joy".

Again, observe as consciousness is drawn from the heart, attracted this time by the mind and its myriad thoughts.

Gently gather the consciousness and lovingly return it back to the heart.

Repeat silently or aloud, "Yoga is the uniting of consciousness in the heart, then I abide in my own true nature, joy".
Observe the movement of consciousness from the heart toward emotions and feelings.

Gently gather the consciousness and lovingly return it back to your heart.

Repeat silently or aloud, "Yoga is the uniting of consciousness in the heart, then I abide in my own true nature, joy".

Gently repeat this sutra any time you notice consciousness moving away from the heart. It will aid you in bringing it back to your heart.

Slowly take in a few deep breaths. Notice how joyful you feel, living from the heart.

It is helpful to practice this for at least ten minutes each day and to repeat the sutra frequently throughout the day, "Yoga is the uniting of consciousness in the heart, then I abide in my own true nature- joy".

Chapter Two

The Eight
Faceted Path

Before beginning any meditation practice it is helpful to understand the path put forth through the Yoga Sutras. The Yoga Sutras offer us **Ashtanga Yoga, the Eight-Faceted Path** a complete system of how to reach the infinite within. Rather than meditation being a solo experience we are shown that it is rather the culmination of the fruits from other practices.

From the Yoga Sutras of Patanjali
The Eight Faceted Path

II-29. Asthaanga Yoga, the Eight-Faceted Path, embraces:

Yama **- Reflection of our true nature**

Niyama **- Evolution toward harmony**

Asana **- Comfort in being, posture**

Pranayama **– Enhancement and guidance of universal** *prana*
(energy)

Pratyahara **– Encouraging the senses to draw within**

Dharana **- Gathering and focusing of consciousness inward**

Dhyana **- Continuous inward flow of consciousness**

Samadhi **- Union with Divine Consciousness**

We find the practical application of Yogic Wisdom distilled into eight dynamic facets. It is so often considered the essence that, for many, the whole study of the sutras is termed *Asthaanga Yoga*.

Asthaanga is two words. *Astha* eight and *angha* intertwining facets. *Angha* is often translated as "limb", and the term can give the impression of a linear ascent, like climbing a tree. Starting at the trunk we wend our way out to the end of the limb. But instead of a completion, the limbs of this tree end in interconnection. This may be frustrating when we are unable to complete each one in its own turn. But it is an integrated system.

Rather than the image of a single tree or limb, the many facets of Asthaanga Yoga are similar to a grove of trees. From the trunk upward, the trees appear to be independent, not connected to each other. However, if we venture several inches below the surface, we will find that these seemingly separate trees have their root systems intertwined.

Their interdependency on each other for enduring strength and drawing in moisture unites them. Each is able to manifest a unique appearance while embracing the same consciousness. Similar to entwined tree roots, we are reminded that Asthaanga is not a series of practices to "accomplish"; rather, it is an offering of infinite possibilities and combinations to enhance our way of being. Because of this we encourage them to interact and function interdependently rather than individually. At times we may choose to single out one or another to help us focus on a particular aspect of our development. After some time, the integration of the other facets will be necessary as we continue our journey inward toward wholeness and discovering our divinity.

Through the process of incarnation our finite bodies must accommodate the vast and infinite ocean of consciousness, as it infuses Divine qualities into our human life. As human beings, we hope to reflect the higher states of consciousness along with our humanity. The Eight-Faceted Path encourages that integration.

The first two facets of Asthaanga *Yoga, Yama* (reflection of our true nature) and *Niyama* (evolution toward harmony) help us purify and align our values with the ultimate goal of spiritual realization.

Within each of these two facets, *Yama* and *Niyama,* there are five additional facets encouraging us to live in peace honoring the spirit at each moment. When we revere all as ourselves through *Ahimsa*, and honor the other four facets of *Yama, Satya* (truthfulness), *Ashteya* (generosity), *Brahmacharya (*moderation), and *Aparigraha* (awareness of abundance) we reflect our True Nature.

Iswara Pranidhana, wholehearted dedication to the Divine, adds radiance to the four other *Niyamas, Saucha* (simplicity), *Santosha* (contentment), *Tapas* (igniting the purifying flame), and *Swadhaya* (sacred study*)*. The integration of the *Yamas* and *Niyamas* in our lives will reproduce its own beauty and light.

The first five facets (*yama, niyama, asana, pranayama, pratytyhara*) are more external than the last three. This structure is meant to suggest that *Dharana* (contemplation), *Dhyana* (meditation) and *Samadhi* (union with divine consciousness) are not practices in themselves, but states that blossom through the nurturing practices that preceded them.

The Yoga Sutras define these three distinct phases of meditation that exhibit a *quantitative* rather than *qualitative* difference. The same attention and awareness that is present in *Dharana* (contemplation) is also brought to *Dhyana* (meditation) and the lower states of *Samadhi* (Union with the Divine). The different phases are determined by the length of time our consciousness is able to remain engaged within.

Imagine this process similar to applying oil to a tough piece of leather, so that it may become supple. The length of time the oil is allowed to remain on the leather is crucial to the process. For it to soak in and soften the leather, it is best to leave it on for a long time. If the oil is applied and then removed within 20 seconds, the softening effect is minimal. If it stays for two minutes, the absorption process is able to begin. When the oil remains on the leather for half an hour or longer, it is completely absorbed, leaving the leather pliable and without a residue.

This is similar to the way *Dharana*, (contemplation), *Dhyana* (meditation) and *Samadhi* (union with the Divine Consciousness) respectively affect the realization of our Divine Self. As we are able to gather our awareness and engage it within for a short amount of time, we are practicing *Dharana*. If engaged for a longer time, we experience *Dhyana*. Yet more time allows for total absorption, *Samadhi*.

Prana
Asana   } HATHA
Pratyhara

From the Yoga Sutras of Patanjali

lll-1 Gathering consciousness and focusing it within is *Dharana (contemplation).*

Dharana is most commonly translated as "concentration" and is frequently used synonymously and interchangeably with the word "meditation". Defining it as concentration suggests an intense focusing of the mind. This characterization can cause our bodies to tense and our breathing to become irregular; and, while our senses are alerted to the mission at hand, there is little comfort or ease. More accurately, *Dharana* invites us into an easeful awareness that prompts the flow of consciousness to return back to its source. In choosing an English equivalent for *Dharana*, "contemplation" or "reflection" is more in keeping with the effect we want to evoke.

Through *Dharana,* our thoughts, feelings and actions interweave, inducing a pattern of consciousness that flows harmoniously to the source.

III-2 The continuous inward flow of consciousness is Dhyana (meditation).

With continued inward awareness, *Dharana* (contemplation) transports us into *Dhyana* (meditation).

In *Dharana* (contemplation) the length of time consciousness dwells with the Divine is limited to a few seconds, causing the sense of peace we derive from *Dharana* to be transient. In *Dhyana (meditation)*, the gathered consciousness nestles more comfortably into our Divine essence.

The distinction between the two stages is similar to the action of a thick liquid (awareness) being poured from a small vessel (*chitta*) back into the infinite sea (*chit*). *Dharana*, intermittently touches inner awareness, similar to the way the liquid pours from a *full* cylinder, stopping ever so briefly before the next plop follows. There is a definite start and end to the periods of inner awareness, and often they happen so quickly that we miss the experience.

Because of these frequent fluctuations in the state of *Dharana*, our awareness vacillates from the external to the internal, between "doing" and "being", back and forth. *Dhyana* (meditation) is analogous to the heavy liquid (awareness) flowing in a *continuous* stream from the small vessel (*chitta*) back to the infinite (*chit*) sea of consciousness. With *Dhyana,* the awareness remains within for a longer time. This allows our identification with the Divine to increase. Even when the "formal" meditation is completed, a part of us is always rooted within.

Dhyana propels our consciousness toward the vast sea of the Divine. Less determined thoughts and emotions are coaxed to flow with it toward the source. This dynamic experience of meditation brims over, touching every aspect of life. The aura (*pranic* body) becomes luminous with this dynamic power, giving you a magnetic and vibrant personality. As this power continues to deepen, people are drawn to you and are affected by your cheerfulness, your immeasurable energy and your joy. Your peace and strength are elevated by the boundless source that you have accessed.

The unpleasant situations that you once avoided are now understood, and in some cases welcomed. You are able to observe that all things have a greater purpose, even if that purpose is sometimes hidden. People you once experienced as foreign or strange now are embraced by your open and loving heart. A whole new perspective has unfolded.

The state of *Dhyana* expands our understanding of the world around us, and of ourselves. We are able to delight in the newfound bliss that up to this time had been held in reserve. In *Dhyana* we transcend the physical, mental and emotional realms, as we experience infinite joy.

III-3 When individual consciousness unites with the Divine Consciousness, the illusion of separateness dissolves; this is Samadhi.

The world that we visit during *Samadhi* (union with the Divine) has no tangible language. It is a state beyond description. It can only be experienced.

If we stir a cup of sugar into a pitcher of water, it *seems* to disappear. We may not be able to *see* it; yet, if we *taste* the water, we recognize the sugar by its sweetness. Because the sugar has been completely absorbed in the water, their union creates a new expression. From then on it becomes impossible to separate the two.

The effect of the sugar merging with water is similar to our gathered consciousness merging into the Divine. When consciousness unites in *Samadhi*, unlike *Dharana* (contemplation) or *Dhyana* (meditation), the distinction between the individual consciousness *(chitta)* and the eternal consciousness *(chit)* dissolves.

Trying to comprehend *Samadhi* (union with the divine) before we have experienced it is like trying to understand being in love before it happens. A child might ask her mother what it feels like to be "in love". With great introspection, her mother may answer, "It is not something that can be explained in words. It is beyond our understanding of what joy can mean. All I can say is you will know it when it happens!" *Samadhi* is like that.

Only in the final phase of *Samadhi*, are our thoughts and mind steadied forever. One part of us always remains with our true self. The Bhagavad-Gita says, "The hand stays in society while the heart rests with the Divine."

With all of our energy focused, the other thousands of thoughts and emotions become impotent. We are able to move past the mind and emotions to experience our center, a completeness. Our true nature shines through.

A MEDITATIVE EXPERIENCE

The Flow from Dharana (contemplation), to Dhyana (meditation) Leading to Samadhi (union with the divine self)

Assume a comfortable and relaxed sitting position. Have the base of the spine directed toward the earth, while the top of the head reaches in the direction of the heavens.

Choose an inspirational object for Dharana (contemplation) something or someone that your heart embraces. It could be your sweetheart, child, parent, a friend, a statue, picture or photo or anything that embodies the essence of Divinity for you. It is effective as long as it uplifts you and allows for an all-encompassing pathway to love.

Begin to inwardly or outwardly observe all the qualities your senses can elicit.

What are you seeing? Beauty, grace, colors, tones, shapes?

What are you touching? Is it soft, smooth, rounded, sensual, solid?
What are you hearing? Is it gentle, strong, inviting, mesmerizing?

What fragrance is enticing you? Is it sweet, fresh, feminine, masculine,
flowery, celestial?

Is your sense of taste involved, perhaps with a kiss?

When you feel the presence of the object of devotion, are you peaceful,
happy, joyous, loving?

Allow the physical eyes to close and begin to cuddle up to all the
sensory experiences now residing deep within your mind and heart.
Embrace the person or the Divine object completely as you encircle it
with a feeling of infinite love.

This experience will escort you to the state of Dharana
(contemplation).

If your heart forgets to embrace your beloved within, notice how your
consciousness wanders away. At these times refresh your thoughts and
feelings by either gazing outward or by reforming a clear image within,
involving all the senses.

The state of Dharana (contemplation) holds only as long as you can
stay present.

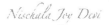

After a period of time (minutes, hours, days, weeks, maybe months or longer), the individual sensory perceptions begin to fade and become less defined. Then the identification with the object and its qualities recedes, and simultaneously a deep feeling of love emerges.

Dharana (contemplation) has merged into Dhyana (meditation).

With the immersion into Dhyana (meditation), the cherished object reveals its essence: all-embracing love. With the unveiling of this knowledge, the indrawn focus becomes effortless.

Continue to dwell at this level of Dhyana (meditation) as the all-embracing love flourishes in your heart.

Now, the threshold into Samadhi (union with the divine) is easily traversed. Any remaining thoughts, feelings and sensory perceptions of the external, now dissolve. Abounding love is your only experience.

With the immersion into Samadhi, your entire reality transforms. You now experience this all-embracing love for everyone and everything.

Chapter Three

❀

Three Characteristics of
Individual Consciousness

Meditation vs
Meditation practice

Through any conditionings, the universal consciousness, or *chit* remains the same. But as our material awareness flourishes, it begins to recede from us. The consciousness we retain is individual consciousness, or *chitta*, which is differentiated into three features: *buddhi, manas,* and *ahamkara.*

Buddhi functions as intellect and intuition, *manas* refers to sense perception, and *ahamkara* is the ego-self perceiving itself as a separate entity. Their cooperation allows us to reason, to perceive the world, to function, and to grow according to our individual needs.

The *buddhi*, as the discriminative and intuitive aspect, has no likes or dislikes. It stores information, and then relays it to the *manas* (senses) or to the *ahamkara* (ego-self). It harmoniously resonates with our inner knowing. The *buddhi* wants and needs nothing for itself and is experienced as a clear reflection of consciousness. (The name *Buddha*, meaning "the enlightened one," is derived from the word *buddhi*.)

The *manas* functions as a receptor of sensual data. Our sight, hearing, taste, touch, and smell are governed by the *manas*. Unable to differentiate on its own, it feeds the sensory information back to the *buddhi* for clarification and validation, or to the *ahamkara* for action.

The *ahamkara* is the sense of "I, me, mine" that is commonly called the ego. This is the part that receives information from the *manas* (senses), and the *buddhi (discrimination)*. It either desires or rejects their findings. "I want that" or "I don't want that." The ego has a poor reputation in spiritual circles as the part of our individual consciousness that divides and separates rather than unifies. In fact, we need a healthy ego to function in the physical world. When the ego is vibrant, it guides us to reflect our true nature, allowing the inner and outer worlds to flow together in harmony. energy

When we delve into the practice of meditation, a yearning for peace and stillness blossoms. The seed, planted long before and hidden deep within, now takes a significant place in our everyday life. Some event has brought it to fruition. It could have been a narrowly escaped accident, an illness, the death of a loved one, a time alone with nature, something that called us from within. Those calls link us with our spiritual selves. We then need to take the time to nurture and water that seed. With zestful and dedicated care, the seed grows and allows us to see the world at many new levels, heights, depths.

As babies, we have few preferences and thought waves; we are contented. We get older and our choices and distinctions multiply: Girls wear pink; boys wear blue. We develop likes and dislikes: Girls like dolls; boys like trucks. You are a good girl if you wear dresses and play with dolls; you are not a good girl if you play with trucks. Our minds and thoughts become polarized, prejudiced. Confusion sets in, and our peace and contentment slowly start to evaporate. We begin to conform *or* rebel, either taking its toll on our quiet minds.

Meditation, while much more than a stress management technique, can be used to relieve and moderate stress. But to use meditation for *only* that purpose is like using a high-powered laser beam to cut bread. Meditation is a tool for *total transformation*. It opens us up to that all-

pervasive feeling of peace, which we may experience as a dynamic stillness.

MAKE THE MIND YOUR FRIEND

When practicing meditation, it's very difficult to gauge yourself or to even measure your *progress* in meditation. The benefits come from the inside and affect the outside. Subtle benefits for a subtle practice.

Don't allow your meditation practice to become a struggle with your mind and emotions. Make them friends, not an enemy. Remember, you, your mind and emotions are on the *same side* — the side of wanting to be calm and peaceful. If the mind and emotions become your enemy, you will never have peace; they will always find a way to agitate you.

As a friend, they will find ways to help you find peace. Instead of *fighting* to control the thoughts and feelings, rise above them as if in an airplane. Get distance from them and look down and see how small and undifferentiated everything looks. Or, if you wish, dive down deep. Like a scuba diver, go below the waves and turbulence to the silence, calmness, and beauty. When our minds become still, we have a clear reflection of what is around us. Go deep within.

Facing a situation that would have upset them previously, people have told me, "Maybe the meditation is doing something after all." They begin to see it with a calmer mind: "It's not worth getting myself all upset over this." "I'm sure there's a way to handle this without getting angry." Sometimes you may *need* to get angry at a particular situation but choose wisely.

This introspection allows you to go beyond the mind and senses and see the *perfection in every act* and act accordingly. These are the kind of "results" to look for.

IS THERE A GOAL FOR MEDITATION?

Meditation is an unusual and somewhat difficult practice for many people, especially in the West. In our culture, our society, we are not rewarded or even encouraged to be still. Many children are told to stop daydreaming and pay attention. Some even have notes sent home from school each report period: "She is a very intelligent student but does not apply herself. She spends her time daydreaming." Children seem to take those breaks naturally. It is a way of taking a "mini vacation" from the place or situation that causes you stress. You may even experience a "mini vacation" at your desk, giving you the needed stillness in the midst of activity. Our society discourages that, calling it *a waste of time*.

Many of us consider our *quiet time* the hours we spend reading newspapers, magazines, and books, watching TV, or listening to music. Our bodies may be still—even calmer than usual—yet our minds may remain very active.

As adults, when we begin to learn to be still and quiet, it is a difficult and sometimes tedious process. At times it seems to be an unnatural process. I want to acknowledge this because it is important not to get discouraged with meditation. Cultivating new habits takes time. Speak to a great singer or pianist. How many years did they practice to become great? How much time did they struggle with their minds?

They probably wanted to do other things instead of practice. Even after they become accomplished, each day they go back to the beginning and practice the scales.

As is often the case with meditation, we think everyone else is easily able to focus and go deep within and that we are the exception. In actuality we are all very much alike, with our minds running here, there, and everywhere.

The mind has been described as a monkey—actually a drunken monkey and not just a drunken monkey, but **a drunken monkey stung by a scorpion**. The mind and emotions tend to dart in many different directions, everywhere except where we want it to be—focused on going inward.

We sometimes feel, "Oh, I've been doing meditation now for two weeks and I've felt nothing." There are many people who have been practicing meditation for twenty and thirty years. They feel benefits on the subtle levels and not necessarily on the physical levels.

When you're calm and quiet, you understand that the world changes. It's the nature of the world to change. It's the nature of the mind and emotions to change. Don't get disillusioned when you do not notice any "effects" from meditation practice.

I befriended a jolly Monk from the Self Realization Center, founded by Paramahansa Yogananda, a great spiritual teacher and one of the early Indian teachers who brought yoga and meditation to the West.

My friend lived at a one of the beautiful shrines the organization provided. Our talks would often venture to Meditation and our experiences.

He related that as a young monk, once a year he would have a private audience with the Master. The routine was the same. He was called into the Master's chambers and was asked how his meditation had been since last visit. Each time he would be a bit embarrassed as he confessed, "Nothing is happening, Master".

He would go on his way with a few encouraging words from his teacher. Finally, after many years of visits and confessions, he had something to tell.

Waiting anxiously, the moment arrived. Jubilantly entering the sacred room, he was ready for the question he usually dreaded.
"Master, this year during my meditations, I started to see lights, and hear sounds. It was incredible to behold."
And as he continued to expound upon his discoveries, he noticed that Yogananadaji was not overly impressed.

At a certain moment the master rose from his seat and came over and touched the monk on the top of his head, with the words." Do not worry it will never happen again"! AND it never did!
"Don't expect flashing lights and bright colors. Don't even expect anything to happen. Meditation is not a circus." -Paramahansa Yogananda,

The experience and effects of meditation is not like physical exercise where you can gage your muscle strength by lifting fifty pounds or more. If you want to see the changes, notice how you react to something that would normally have made you angry. Be pleased when you say, "It's not worth getting upset over that." Or "This too shall pass."

This introspection allows you to go beyond the mind. emotions and senses to recognize the perfection in every act. These are the kind of "results" to look for. It's very hard to gauge yourself, to even measure your progress in meditation. It's something that happens on a very subtle level. It comes from the inside and effects the outside. Please don't get disillusioned.

PRACTICE, PRACTICE, PRACTICE

Sometimes, even when we hear it from an expert, our minds are in doubt. His Holiness the Dalai Lama was holding a retreat for a large group of people. Each day he would lecture on the different aspects of meditation and its presence in daily life. Patiently he would explain that the only way to feel the benefits was to practice, practice, practice. It may take years to experience a sense of peace that permeates our everyday lives.

Each day, before and after his talks, there was a period of meditation. The practice would resume in the evening, after which he would patiently and compassionately answer questions.

One man who had been at the retreat all week raised his hand and asked, "All this takes so long. Isn't there an easier and quicker way to get to this place of peace?"

The Dalai Lama cradled his head in his hands. He remained that way for about five minutes. When he finally raised his head, his face was streaked with tears. His eyes lit upon the many faces in the audience, as if to absorb understanding.

After what seemed like a long time, he began to speak slowly. With his hands balled up into fists, he chanted, "THERE IS NO EASY, QUICK WAY! THERE IS NO EASY, QUICK WAY! THERE IS NO EASY, QUICK WAY!"

Don't give up or get disillusioned with meditation. If you need results, look for long-term results, not quick ones. All great accomplishments take time. By daily, vigilant practice, the benefits will transform your body and mind, to touch the spirit.

Chapter Four

Medicine and Meditation

As medical science studies the effects of meditation on the body we begin to see why many of the ancient sages lived a long healthy life. In meditation the body and the mind become relaxed and efficient.

This has the effect of lowering blood pressure, increasing immune function and allowing us to feel vital and a greater sense of being in control of our lives. The beta waves normally found in the active mind are replaces by calmer alpha waves and with deeper practice even theta waves. The quality of sleep becomes sounder, general well-being and joy for life is fostered. However, remember this practice goes far beyond the physical and even mental realms. It will lead us to permanent peace the Peace that is beyond all understanding.

I was fortunate to be involved in two clinical studies, The Lifestyle Heart Trial and Multi Center Lifestyle Heart Trial, that proved that a Yoga based lifestyle could reverse Cardio-Vascular Disease. It was interesting to note that those who did the most Yoga practice, including meditation, each day had the greatest reversal of their heart disease.

Also being a co-founder of the Commonweal Cancer Help Program, and having worked with many people with Cancer, the practices were found to boost immune function as well as reduce pain.

Perhaps what we're missing in our society is this time of going within, and because of that we're developing many stress-related diseases. Could these diseases be nature's way of drawing us away from the "busyness" of life to take time to be with ourselves again, and to heal?

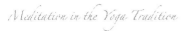

A CASE STUDY

Peg was a nurse and was certain her prognosis was leading her to a swan song. The fear of her family history of breast cancer led her to the drastic act of removing both of her normal breasts. "This is not uncommon," she tried to convince me, "when your mother, sister, aunts, and grandmothers all died of breast cancer. I had it done for my peace of mind."

As it turned out, that even after the radical surgery for breast surgery she developed ovarian cancer. Before it could be diagnosed, it had metastasized to her liver and lungs. Some part of her accepted this as her fate, while another part wished she could extend her shortened life. Her spiritual life became her focus and fervently created a structure for her inner life to emerge. She came to spend time with me because to her *intuitive* self it felt right.

"I know that soon the cancer will take over my whole body and I will die. I am still a physically young woman. I had hoped to see my children grow up. That hope is now gone. I also know that a large part of who I am will live on. Will you help me get more in touch with that spirit within?"

After a few initial sessions in meditation instruction, Peg could be seen sitting on the grass or on her bed until all hours, meditating. It was clear by the feeling surrounding her that she was touching deep places of comfort and healing.

One early morning she gave a perfunctory knock on my door and without waiting for an affirmative answer, she burst into my room. Sitting on my bed, she was wide-eyed and wild. "What is it? What happened?" my voice croaked from sleep as much as surprise.

"I just retrieved an experience from somewhere deep in me that I had forgotten or buried, so horrific that every part of my body, mind, and soul are shaken." I sat up and braced myself for the energy and words of the event.

Her boyfriend was going to visit some friends in a city two thousand miles away. He had left early one morning while she was still in bed, half asleep. With a promise to call that night, he planted a kiss on her lips and was off.

Late that night a phone call came. It was not as she had expected. About seven that night, she fell into a swoon. All the physical world suddenly became translucent; she was seeing through the veils. Feeling a sense of unease, she could "see" her beloved sitting in a strange place.

Suddenly there was a gun pointing at him, with first one, then another explosion. He was gripping his belly and his pain was *their* pain. She felt it as a hot iron, bursting inside her belly, ripping at her insides.

Fear, panic, and horror kept her paralyzed until the ringing of the phone wrenched her back to a solid physical form. The voice at the other end said that her boyfriend had been shot and killed by two bullets in the abdomen. She replaced the phone and closed a heavy curtain to the pain and memory of that horrid scene.

Peg had trusted the curtain to keep the pain from her and she had not remembered anything about that night for five years. Now, as she delved into the recesses of her soul, she found a monster that was unknowingly gnawing away at her day and night. This realization was like discovering a new part of her that she had forgotten existed. She was meeting a long-lost friend who had suffered much—the fear, the crying, the awe of it.

The physical and emotional integration of this event was both difficult and easy at the same time. Slowly owning the experience as an important part of her emotional and spiritual life, Peg continued to practice meditation. She was getting to know *all* of herself, perhaps for the first time in many years.

A few months later I received a phone call.

"Have you heard about Peg?"

"No," I said preparing for the worst.

"Well, she went to see her doctor and she is completely free of any cancer. It is gone. She has had a complete, unexplained, spontaneous remission from her disease!"

What *actually* healed Peg we may never know. It is one of those situations we hesitate to call a miracle because we want the unseen higher power to remain *anonymous*.

I later found out that there are more than fifty thousand such *unexplained* spontaneous remissions each year in the United States that are *reported*. We don't know how many happen to people who just never tell anyone. A doctor may tell her patient to go home and make arrangements to die. Two years later she sees them in the supermarket buying zucchini! The curious part is that no one in the *medical* community can explain it. It seems to have some correlation with going deep within. Something amazing happens when we touch the divine spirit.

Chapter Five

How to Choose a Focus for Meditation

THE STATE OF MEDITATION

Meditation is a state reached at the culmination of Yoga Practice. *Dharana* (contemplation), *Dhyana* (meditation) and *Samadhi*, (absorption) are considered states of being rather than practices. They are not something that we *do or even practice*. We use techniques to get us to the point of meditation or stillness. Once we get to that point we are no longer *doing,* we just *are*.

Beginning practice, we often expect to be able to just stop or immediately control our thoughts, emotions or senses. In frustration, we say, "I can't stop my thoughts or emotions." Thoughts and emotions have run wild for our whole life, yet we expect, with one or two sessions, for them to obediently come under control.

In meditation thoughts and emotions float by. We come to understand that most of what we think, and feel are not that important in the vast scheme of life. Most of what we project never happens anyway. Of all the plans we make, half of them never happen. Of all the worrying we do, most of that never happens either. Why waste that time? We experience frustration and a feeling that we are the only ones in the world unable to control their thoughts. So, pull back from life's trials, watch them, and if you can, laugh at them.

Begin to observe the mind and thoughts as if they were projected on a movie screen. When one initially walks into a movie theater, there is only a plain white screen. Then suddenly the lights dim, and something is projected on the blank screen, we are instantly drawn into the drama. Just as the scenes in a movie change, so do our thoughts and emotions.

In the end, we realize that *life* like a movie, is just a *projection* from our mind.

A great spiritual teacher wanted to prove this very point to his students. He took a group of them to see a very scary movie. When they entered the theater the movie screen was a shiny white blank. The teacher took his place in the row behind the students so he could observe them. "Now remember," he said, "this is just a movie."

"Oh, yes, we know," they repeated, "this is just a movie."

The movie began to fill the white screen with action. As it progressed, the frightening scenes came and the teacher observed the students leaning forward in their seats, tensing their bodies, some with frightened looks on their faces. The teacher then let out a roar of laughter. "Ha, ha, ha. You forgot. It is just a movie." As the remembrance came they relaxed back in their chairs. Again, a few minutes later, they would forget and become tense again, and on and on it went. At the end of the movie, the screen went once again turned plain white and the lights went on. It *was* a movie after all!

Our main objective in life is to remember—remember who we are in the midst of all the "busyness" of the outer world *and* our inner worlds. When we look toward finding a meditation practice, *The Yoga Sutras of Patanjali* are very empowering and nonrestrictive.

Mantra (mind control)
Mudras —> Leap —> Meditation
Japa   OR
          Bridge

From the Yoga Sutras of Patanjali

I-39 Dedicate yourself to anything that elevates and embraces your heart.

The sutras offer a few suggestions for choosing a focus for meditation; they then give us *carte blanche* to choose anything to which we want to dedicate our hearts. Religious and spiritual traditions have generously offered us many wonderful suggestions for focusing the mind and heart. Many people will find a suitable choice from within that group. If you do not find one that unlocks *your* heart, the sutras now invite you to create your own.

They simply suggest using two guiding principles for selecting an object of focus to lead us to higher consciousness. First, choose something that will elevate the heart and mind just by invoking its presence. And second, choose something that you love dearly and embrace it fully in your heart. If you are sincere and dedicated, you will be transported to its Divine qualities and from there your inner peace will be unveiled. These are sure recipes for success in spiritual practice.

CHOOSING A PRACTICE

In choosing an object for meditation we look for something that uplifts and inspires us. It can be something in nature, perhaps remembering a time you stood transfixed looking at a sunset. So, taken by its beauty that you were barely breathing? Or sitting in front of a roaring fire captured by the warmth and radiance? Or even a great soul whose life we admire.

Many of us have had the experience of falling in love. How our whole world and attention is geared to that one person all of our senses, our thoughts are with him or her and that uplifts us and makes us happy. When choosing a technique also feel that same one-pointed devotion. Choose something that makes you feel happy, that you like very much.

We are less likely to be distracted if we really like the technique. When distractions occur such as discomfort in the knee or a should do in the mind-just observe it acknowledge it and bring the mind back to the focus. If the distraction persists, make an arrangement that you will do the appropriate action as soon as the meditation is finished. If the distraction still persists-see to the distraction i.e. move the knee slightly jot down the thought and return undisturbed to the object of meditation. The more you draw inward the less distractions will appear.

When choosing a practice for yourself or others, be certain that it is part of their cherished belief system. If possible, keep it simple.
A friend of mine who has a longtime career as a cardiac surgeon went on a ten-day meditation retreat. When he returned, I asked him how the experience had been for him. "Oh, it was fine," he answered, still somewhat preoccupied. "Tell me something," he said. "They told us to meditate on the *hara* [an energy center used in Buddhist meditation]. I spent the whole time trying to figure out exactly where it was. Using my memory, I went through my copy of *Gray's Anatomy,* but I couldn't figure out if it is to the left or right of the pancreas, above or below it. Can you help clarify it for me?"

Half chuckling to myself and at the same time appreciating his dilemma, I said, "Let's make this easy. Do you know where your heart is?" "Of course, I know where my heart is—and everybody else's, too," answered the experienced surgeon. "Put your full and complete attention at the heart, with all the love that flows through it. That is a grand object for meditation," I said. He looked relieved and a slight smile appeared in his sparkling eyes.

It is important where we place our focus for Meditation. It varies with the individual as you can see from the story. There are two main focuses recommended and many others that may come naturally.

When we place the awareness at the *Ajna Chakra*, the third eye in the middle of the forehead, the eyes tilt slightly upward toward the inner light. This seems to be a comfortable positioning as the eyes naturally gaze upward when they close. It directs the energy upward, toward the infinite.

The other place recommended for focus is the *Anahatha Chakra*, or Heart Center. Directing the awareness to the heart is always a good choice. It is also a great focus if you are practicing meditation on or with the breath. The heart can be observed in the same in and out flow as the breath as in giving and sending out love. Focusing on the heart brings us back to the universal love held in our hearts.

Either place is effective in keeping the awareness from roaming. And both elevate us to the highest consciousness.

When you actually select an object for meditation, choose one you feel a certain one-pointed devotion towards. Sometimes, in our impatience, we feel, *Oh, this technique is not working*. We speak to a friend or read a book about a certain method and decide to change ours. This is often the grass is always greener approach.

Give your chosen practice time to go deep. There's an adage about digging shallow wells that seems to apply to this. If you are trying to get water, you may start on a particular spot and dig down ten feet.

When no water comes forth you may try again in another place, go down another ten feet but this time you hit rock. You continue to the next place and again go ten feet down and you still are not getting water. You could keep digging many ten-foot holes and never reach water. But if you dig only one well and dig thirty or forty feet straight down, there is a better chance, you will eventually get water.

By switching techniques back and forth, you're not getting the depth and steadiness needed. It is like buying a fire extinguisher and each week moving it to a different place. When the fire comes, you will not remember where to look.

Embrace one practice that is the closest to your temperament. Date it for a while. You don't have to get married to it, but at least keep steady company. Then, if you decide in three or four weeks that it is not for you, select another. Stay with that one for a month or so. After two or three tries, choose one and make your marriage plans. Apply that devotion to your meditation and go deep within. Becoming familiar with your chosen practice allows you to move more quickly to the quiet and stillness within.

Is it beneficial to keeping the technique sacred and not speaking about it to others? Some say yes, while others laugh at the idea. Yet, if we cherish and value an object it becomes special and even sacred. Let's say we were having a nice visit and I pull a gold and emerald ring out of a popcorn box. Would you doubt it was real? On the other hand, if I invited you into my room and closed the door, then unlocked a drawer and took out a velvet box, you might anticipate an expensive jewel. Much of our regard comes from our intention. If we feel we have chosen a special and very powerful meditation practice, it will be so.

DOES ONE NEED A TEACHER OR GURU?

From the Yoga Sutras of Patanjali

L.25 The Divine is the essence of all knowledge, wisdom, and love.

L.26 Knowledge, wisdom, and love are the omnipresent teachers, in all beings.

Does one need a teacher or *Guru* to meditate or progress in the spiritual path? There are two distinct opinions. One will say, a *Guru* is necessary as Yoga has for millennia been a tradition that directly transmits the power of its teachings from *guru* to disciple. Then the disciple becomes the Guru and transmits to the student and the cycle continues. A *guru* can also be the source of your devotion.

Others say a Guru is not necessary as the knowledge is within. While I agree with both views, it can be very helpful to have a guide.

I have been fortunate to have been with many teachers. However, I have only had a few Gurus. Sri Swami Satchidanandaji, a great spiritual master originally from India was the one I embraced to form my path and guide me for many years. I found this invaluable, and even to this day I cherish his enlightened guidance. I recognize this is not for everyone and not always available. Keep an open heart and mind and at some point, the *Guru* may appear.

"When the student is ready the Guru appears."

Finding a true teacher in the uncharted territory of spirituality is challenging. Especially in these more skeptical times, the value of a living teacher is not appreciated. A true *Sat Guru* does not merely pass on her or his acquired knowledge; the *guru* also transmits *shakti* (energy) from her or his vast reserves, to help kindle our own spark.

Choosing the right teacher is not always as easy as we would like. Place integrity at the top of the list when looking for a spiritual teacher. Many spiritual teachers by their actions reflect the teachings back to us. They show us who we truly are *and* the greatness that is our essential nature. Some show through their actions *exactly what you do not want to become*. Both are valuable. Much is reported these days about *gurus* demanding that their students live an exemplary life, one that they themselves do not live. Before placing your total faith in a spiritual teacher, examine closely how she or he embodies the worldly and Divine traits you wish to emulate.

Another important aspect is to always seek out a teacher who wants you to outshine them, not one who hopes to keep you in the student role forever. Learn as much from the guru on as many levels of your being as you are able. Let her or him be the link that will take you back to the essence of all teachings: the light within your own heart. When that spark is ignited, a true *Sat Guru* will be clear in letting you know that is not her or his light that s/he has given to you; instead, s/he has assisted you in rediscovering the same light of the Divine that shines in all. The purpose of seeking and learning from a *guru* is not to be bound, but to be *free*.

I have added a worthwhile addition to the adage above.
"When the student is ready the *guru* appears." will eventually become:
"When the student is ready the *guru* disappears!"

MAY THE GURU BE WITH YOU WHEREVER YOU ARE!

It is not always necessary for the *guru* or teacher to be in physical proximity or even in the physical form to impart their *shakti*. Many evolved souls guide us from other physical locations and subtle realms. The subtle knows no boundaries. Spiritual support can come from the next town or from the far-reaching vistas we are yet to explore. For example, Lord Jesus, Lord Buddha, Lord Siva, Allah, Sri Krishna, or Sri Radha, Sri Durga, Sri Lakshmi, Kwan Yin, Mother Mary as well as many other enlightened teachers have successfully inspired devotees to find their Divine essence for millennia. This is why the sutras say that the teacher of all teachers, the *guru* of all *gurus* is knowledge, wisdom, and love, boundless, eternal, pure, and unchanged by time.

You are my mother, father, sister, brother
friend, you are my all light of light
Oh light of lights

A MEDITATIVE EXPERIENCE

Your Relationship to the Internal or External Guru

Sit quietly and allow yourself to recall all the gurus and teachers who have taught you in the past and those who are guiding you now.

What lessons have you learned?
How to act and how to be?

Were there some that showed you, by their words or actions, what not to do and how not to be?

Observing your present spiritual path, could a guru or a teacher enrich and increase the depth of your practice?

The first step in attracting a guru or a teacher is knowing that you are ready to receive guidance.

Set the intention and open your heart.

If you already have a guru or a teacher, are you able to accept the teachings wholeheartedly?

Does the guru or teacher live what s/he teaches?

Does s/he allow you to grow and flourish in your own personality?

Recommit yourself to, knowledge, wisdom and love as the ultimate teachers.

DISTRACTIONS IN MEDITATION

How many of us are accustomed to sitting still and at least outwardly do nothing? It is not part of our society and our western heritage. We are taught to always be doing something. In some cases, we even do more than one or even two things at a time. How many of us eat and read or watch TV or all three? Meditation is the ability to focus on one point and then allow that one pointedness to filter into other aspects of our everyday life. To only eat when we eat, when we speak to only speak, simple yet difficult to do.

At first when sitting still you may observe aches and pains and stiffness you never knew were there. It is very helpful to have a regular daily routine of gentle stretching to help alleviate the discomfort. A little stretching first can make a big difference in your ability to be still. Without a still body the mind cannot be still.

We all have busy lives—filled with lists, time commitments, and too little time to do them. With all the busyness it often is difficult to be still. When we try to sit for meditation the body could summon the awareness for attention. Or when the body becomes still all the thoughts and emotions come rushing to the forefront of our minds. There are three main ways to dispel these distractions, that come and demand our attention.

Sometimes it is easier to observe how our adult mind works by observing small children. They have not yet learned to cloak their ways as adults have. In the quiet of meditation, our minds tend to lose their cloaking device and become as transparent as when we were children.

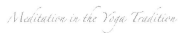

See if you can relate the obstacles that occur during meditation to this observation of small children.

#1 Distraction

As her mother talked with a friend, Clara's daughter felt ignored, left out. She interrupted the conversation, "Excuse me, Mommy. Mommy, Mommy, excuse me, Mommmmmy."

The first thing Clara did was try to ignore the interruption. That is also the first thing to do with a distraction in meditation. For instance, your back hurts. That's a common complaint. You're sitting quietly and you've gotten yourself really comfortable. You think, *I'm going to sit for fifteen minutes without moving*. Then your body says, *Oh, yeah? That's what you think! Okay, back, do your job: Start to ache and distract her*.

The obedient *back* goes toward an Academy Award for Best Performance by an Aching Back. Trying to ignore it we think, *I'm focusing on* [whatever your meditation technique is]. *I hear the back calling, but I'm not going to pay any attention to it*. That is the first step.

#2 Distraction

A child might go away at this point, but most of the time, they're more tenacious than that. Instead of just saying, "Mommy, Mommy," the child will start pulling on you, tugging on you, getting a little louder. At that point, your friend Clara may take a moment break from the conversation, "Excuse me," as she turns toward the child, and says, "Not now, honey. I'll talk to you a little later. I'm speaking with Susan right now." Clara's still calm and she didn't lose too much awareness of the conversation; instead she just dealt with the interruption quickly. If you observe the same type of distractions, make an agreement with yourself to attend to the *urgent* situation as soon as your meditation is finished. That's the second way you can deal with a distraction.

#3 Distraction

Some children decide to be very loud and even have a tantrum. (Some backs may decide to do that too!) As you're meditating, you experience the back is still hurting. Speaking gently to the back "*Okay, I'll stretch in just a little bit. Then I want you to be quiet after that.*"

The mind now gets a bit more assertive and tries to convince you that if you do not move right now, all the blood will stop flowing to it, which will cause permanent damage and you may never be able to sit again. In that case, you realize that the mind will not stop until it has distracted you completely. You stop meditating for a moment and briefly stretch, reposition your back or place a pillow in a strategic spot. Make a promise that when you are finished you will soak in a tub or rub some oil on your back or give it whatever it needs. Then find your way back to the inward place of meditation.

Not all the distractions are physical; some are mental or emotional: "I thought of something and I know that if I don't write it down right this minute it will go out of my mind completely and that million dollars I could make will never happen." That's how forthright the thoughts get in meditation. The stronger they are, the more power they have to distract. Have a pad and pencil beside you, and if you get any *brilliant* thoughts, as a final resort, just write them down. I would suggest first trying the ignoring stage and the reasoning stage, then, if necessary, jot it down and say, "All right now, mind, go back to meditation." You will find—upon your return after the distraction—that it is more difficult to concentrate. The same thing happens when we are distracted while having the conversation with a friend: "Now, where was I before the distraction came?"

Know your mind and emotions and be gentle with them. If you have a mind that rebels with "shoulds" and force, use a reward instead of a punishment: "We can take a long walk later," or "We can spend more time talking to our friend over dinner," or whatever is a healthy reward for you. Don't force it or say, "You're going to sit here and you're going to meditate no matter what, young lady. This is good for you!" Most of the time that kind of demand does not work in the long run.

You haven't tried to still the mind, emotions and senses for all these years; now suddenly you expect them to *behave*? Why should they listen to you now? If in first grade we began training —along with learning how to read and write—the mind, emotions and senses they would be calmer and easier to control now. It is the nature of the mind to be tumultuous and our nature to want to control it.

REGULARITY AND DEDICATION-TWO PILLARS

From the Yoga Sutras of Patanjali

I.13 Devoted practice, *Abhyasa*, cultivates the unfolding of consciousness.

I.14 *Abhyasa* is nurtured by a sustained, steady rhythm and a dedicated heart.

Make meditation a good, steady habit. You become well-grounded in practice when it is sustained for a long period of time, with regularity and steadiness, and a dedicated heart.

A long period of time means to do it long enough that it becomes as natural to meditate as it is to talk, walk, and breathe. This is not something easily accomplished in one or two months. Set aside a certain time each day for the practice. Be practical. If you set your goals unrealistically high and cannot fulfill those goals, you feel like a failure. If you set realistic goals, you feel good about meeting them. To begin with, take ten minutes once or twice a day and be true to it. Allow it to become a *good* habit. After a while—maybe in a month or more—if you have kept to the ten minutes regularly, add five more minutes to the practice time, slowly and steadily building a strong structure.

When you sit, make a firm affirmation or intent (*sankulpa*) I'm going to sit for fifteen minutes every morning and evening. No matter what happens during that time, no matter what I think of as important, I'm going to sit without moving. You can even add a particular time of the day: eight o'clock every morning or six o'clock every evening.

Have each day beat with a rhythmical and regular meditation routine, a routine that becomes as much a part of your day as getting up and brushing your teeth. Would you think of going out without brushing your teeth or washing your face? It's not the way most of us were taught. In that same way make meditation a new good habit. Get up, brush your teeth, wash your face, and meditate. Come back from work, meditate, eat dinner, go to sleep. It becomes a natural progression. If for some reason you don't meditate on a particular day, you may not feel quite right—just like you don't feel clean if you forget to brush your teeth or wash your face. One is a cleansing of the body, the other a cleansing of the mind and emotions.

We come up with creative interpretations as to what a sustained, steady practice might be. I heard a Yoga teacher tell her students that four or five times a week is enough. In my experience the four or five times whittles down three or four times and then one or two which then fades into zero. "I don't need to do it on my vacation when I am relaxed, do I?" With a less busy schedule, we are able to do *more* on holidays and days off, the opposite of time off for good behavior. More time for meditation helps encourage our *best* behavior.

The next aspect is to understand what is meant by a dedicated heart. It is a deep *love* for the practice. Remember, when we love something, we embrace it with our *whole heart*.

A student of the great teacher. Sri Ramakrishna, asked what it would that feel like to be dedicated to his practice? Without speaking, the teacher simply motioned for the student to follow him to the lake.

Directing the student to enter the water, the teacher followed. Deeper and deeper they went. Finally, when they were shoulder-deep in water, the teacher placed his hand on the student's head and pushed him under the water. Somewhat relaxed, the student felt trust and excitement, anticipating a secret initiation. After some time, the need for air won out over the other expectation. Flailing arms and legs, the student struggled for that precious breath. He was unable to move. Desperate, the student—with all his might—pushed himself up just as the teacher pulled him out of the water.

"What," asked the teacher, "were you thinking about while under the water?"

Still gasping for breath, the student exclaimed one word: "Air!"

"Anything else?" the teacher asked.

"Air was the only thing I wanted! It was the only thing I could think of."

"Indeed," smiled Sri Ramakrishna, "when you want to know your divine self as much as you wanted that air, then you shall have it."

When all three criteria— a sustained, steady rhythm and a dedicated heart —are met, we feel a natural flow with our spirit.

CREATING A SACRED PLACE

Create a special place that inspires you to set aside a certain time each day for meditation practice. It is best to choose a time you feel fully awake and the stomach is light. Do not allow the world to permeate that place. No phone. no thoughts or worries. Have a special pillow or chair, a blanket, a candle, an inspirational book anything uplifting to encourage you to sit and be still. Just as we may not feel hungry until we step into the kitchen, seeing our meditation place can also entice us feel the hunger for peace.

Create a sacred place in your home that draws you in and inspires you to spend time each day in meditation. It can be a corner of a room or if possible, an entire room, that is dedicated to experiencing your inner self. In that sacred place, have everything you need for practice. A cushion or chair, a blanket or shawl, a listening device and a few inspirational books make the space inviting.

It is helpful to set up an altar to create a focus that holds and then transmits a powerful vibration. This will attract you to that sacred place for meditation. Place your most inspiring pictures be they of teachers, an aspect of nature or anything uplifting. If possible, position the altar so as you sit facing the altar you are looking either **East** or **North**.

Have all five of the natural elements represented on the altar. For **Earth**, a flower, crystal or plant. For **Water**, a photo of river or the ocean, a small bowl of water or a vase with fresh flowers. For **Fire**, a candle or light: **Air** and **Ether** could be represented by a bell, a chime or incense. Use any items that evoke the peace and joy in your heart.

Most rooms in our homes have specific purposes. The bedroom is for sleeping and resting. The bathroom for cleansing. The kitchen is for preparing and eating food. Often passing through the kitchen even if we are not hungry, the vibration of food will entice us to eat a "little something". In a similar way experiencing our sacred place can entice us to "sit for just a few minutes". It will remind you each time you pass, to reacquaint yourself with the peace within. Do not allow the world to permeate your special place not even friendly, intruders. Leave all worldly thoughts or worries behind as you open to the peace within.

Chapter Six

Preparing the Body for Meditation

From the Yoga Sutras of Patanjali

ll-46 The natural comfort and joy of our being is expressed when the body becomes steady (*asana*).

II-47 As the body yields all efforts and holdings, the infinite within is revealed.

II-48 Thereafter we are freed from the fluctuations of the *Gunas*.

We now venture to the more physical aspects of *Asthaangha Yoga* known as *Hatha Yoga*. Their positioning after *Yama* and *Niyama* suggests that embracing a high level of behavior *before* beginning *asana, pranayama and pratyahara* practice protects us from misusing or wasting the very powerful energy that is released. When we are firmly grounded in these principles, any unseemly thoughts or emotions are neither exacerbated nor strengthened during the practices of *Hatha Yoga*.

The complete system of *Hatha Yoga* increases vital energy by aligning our physical and subtle bodies, through physical poses (*asana*), guiding and enhancing the life force through breathing practices (*pranayama*) and encouraging the senses to draw inward (*pratyahara*). All three aspects were designed to be practiced in concert, thereby harmonizing body, breath and senses.

When popularized in the West, the physical postures (*asana*) were isolated, excluding the other two aspects of *Hatha Yoga* almost completely. This oversight can encourage imbalances and injuries to the body, as well to as the mental and emotional wellbeing. Today,

After - 5 element earth, water, fire, air, ether

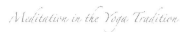

most people commonly refer to the isolated practice of *asana* as the total system, simply calling it **Yoga**.

HA-THA, A BALANCE OF ENERGIES

Ha-tha represents the integrated energy that then polarizes within each of us as light and dark, sun and moon, masculine and feminine. *Ha* represents the sun, heating, and "masculine" qualities of reason and intellectual thinking. *Tha* characterizes the moon, exhibiting coolness and the "feminine" qualities of emotion and intuition. Each one of us has both the male *Ha* and the female *tha* within us in varied proportions. The finer the balance, the more harmonious we feel.

When describing *Asana*, Sutra II-46 uses two Sanskrit words: *Sthira* and *Sukha*.

Sthira denotes an effortlessness while coming into a pose, through the process of holding steady and remains present as the body returns to relaxation.

Sukha reflects the body experiencing its natural state of comfort and joy. As the body becomes easeful, the mind and emotions align with it, reflecting the Divine Light within. The inner and outer worlds interconnect and harmonize.

THREE ASPECTS OF NATURE THE THREE GUNAS

According to Yoga all of nature, reflects a predominance of one of three attributes. These attributes are called *Tri (three) Gunas (attribute* of nature): sattwa, balance; rajas, activity-over activity; and tamas, inactivity-inertia. The world and everything in it constantly move between these three attributes of nature. Much like a seesaw. There's overactivity on one side, underactivity on the other, and when both are equal there is balance.

During the day (rajas), the light is strong; we are outward and active. At night (tamas), the light is withdrawn; we become more indrawn and quieter. At the moment when day merges into night and night merges into day, there is balance (sattwa). Perhaps this is why dawn and dusk are observed by many traditions as auspicious times for prayer and meditation, a time of equanimity. This balance of nature is what we hope to attain for our bodies and minds through Hatha Yoga practices.

The Sutras on Asana offer the assurance that as we calm the body, all the Gunas will cease to fluctuate. We are then freed from all earthly restraints enabling us to move our consciousness upward to the world of spirit.

The placement of the sutras on Hatha Yoga at the threshold of Dharana, Dhyana and Samadhi suggests they are a preparation for sitting meditation. Aching bodies distracted the ancient yogis in their quest to sit still. Reflecting the disturbances in their body, mind or emotions they became restless. Unable to dedicate their focus inward, they realized that settling the mind and emotions was unlikely if even the slightest distraction remained in the body.

This seems even more vital today in the modern world. All the disturbances are perpetuated by the attributes of Nature or the *Three Gunas*.

By practicing a few simple *asanas* or poses *before* sitting, a sense of comfort and ease in the body is encouraged, the mind and emotions calm, and the spirit is more readily accessed. After all, a certain amount of discipline and physical strength is needed to keep the body in a steady seated position without movement for a half-hour or longer. Through *asana* practice, distractions of the body become infrequent visitors. The result is that we feel better, look better, and can project that feeling into our daily life.

Today there are hundreds of methods and schools for practicing *Yoga asanas*. Choose the type of asana you want to practice, based, not just on the physical benefits but also on how it will affect your mental and emotional makeup. It is essential to understand what type of practice your particular temperament requires. Also, be aware of the effect that the practice is having on the subtle nervous system. If your nervous system is sensitive and you adapt a vigorous *asana* practice, it may cause imbalance. Allow *asana* to be **one** part of your complete *Hatha Yoga* practice.

Keep the goal of stillness and steadiness at the forefront of your practice, readying the body to find the comfort of one meditative pose to support a prolonged period of stillness. As the asana practice is established, it affords flexibility of body, mind and emotions. With this comes balance and the yearning to be still and know yourself.

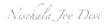

"The body itself is to reveal the light that's blazing inside your Presence." – Rumi

One often asked question is "Why can't I do meditation in a reclining chair or even in bed? Why must I sit with the spine erect?"

We are the connection between the heaven and earth. Through our feet we draw in the earth energy upward as the heaven energy flows downward from the heavens into the crown of our head. These energy currents, flow up and down the spine, conveying the energy from both heaven and earth. To aid us in connecting to the heaven energy, the body must be sitting erect. This encourages the upward flow of energy from the base of the spine. It's very similar to basic physics: Hot air (energy) rises. The difference in temperature in a room can be felt differently if we are sitting on the floor, a chair or standing. In meditation there is a buildup of subtle energy that, if allowed to rise, opens us to places of higher consciousness and awareness. It is from here that our physical, emotional, and mental balance flows. We experience a pleasant distancing from our thoughts, feelings, and even our bodies.

This is all more easily achieved in a sitting position. When lying down as in deep relaxation, the energy tends to dissipate. This posturing allows us to consciously let go of energy so we can relax. Sitting erect with a relaxed body enables us to enter meditation. The focused energy rises up through the *Anahatha Chakra* (heart), the *Vishudda Chakra* (throat), the *Ajna Chakra* (third eye), and continues through *Sahasara*

Chakra (crown). Compassion and discrimination, peace and oneness are our outward rewards.

Have you ever noticed your posture at an important meeting or a lecture? You may be sitting back in your chair, relaxed. Suddenly the topic changes to something that relates to you directly. Perhaps someone has just offered you a four-million-dollar contract. What happens to your posture? It suddenly straightens. You instinctively know that by sitting upright the energy flows upward allowing you to understand, discern, and make the proper judgment. The erect body plays a crucial role in allowing the energy to flow.

There are many wonderful Asanas recommended for meditation, find the one most comfortable to you.

The first two asanas shown below are for beginning meditators or those more experienced that might not have the flexibility or comfort of body to sit in a formal asana on the floor. A chair is a wonderful way to sit still and erect for longer periods. Some prefer a meditation bench, while many will opt for a floor pose. The asanas seated on the floor provide a stability that allows for any quick jolts or movements that sometimes accompanying the energy as it rises in pranayama and meditation. Any position that is comfortable and steady is a great asana.

Below find some of the more traditional asanas recommended for meditation that have been used for thousands of years. Remember chose a position that brings joy and comfortable to your particular body!

SUGGESTED POSTURES FOR MEDITATION

Easy Crosslegged
Sukhasana

Sitting in a Chair

Half Lotus
Ardha Padmasana

Full Lotus
Padmasana

Diamond
Vajrasana

Accomplished
Siddhasana

Let's direct our awareness to the posture. Most importantly, sit comfortably with the back erect. If you are seated on a chair have the feet crossed at the ankles or flat on the floor. If you choose to sit on the floor crossed legged or against the wall with the legs stretched out, have a firm pillow under the buttocks and if against the wall a pillow supporting the lower back.

Some people prefer sitting on a meditation bench with the legs folded under them. Many who begin cross legged on the floor because of books or photos they have seen in that position, quickly realize that it is a skill that may take some time to develop. Experiment to see what is most comfortable for you.

Have the arms resting gently on the legs with the palms up in a receiving position. Touch the thumb and forefinger together or have the hands resting one over the other in your lap thumbs touching. Whichever hand position you choose be sure that the shoulders are back and relaxed which allows the spine to remain erect.

Observe the spine supporting you from the base to the top where the head perfectly balances on its perch. Feel each vertebra as it supports and lifts you upward. Since our state of mind is reflected in our bodies and especially in our faces allow the jaw to be relaxed, the chin level, the face soft with a slight smile. This helps to reflect both inward and outward contentment.

The eyes may be closed or open. If the mind is very active or perhaps you feel as if you are closer to sleep than meditation try having the eyes slightly open and gazing downward. As the mind quiets you may allow the eyes to close. It is interesting to notice when the mind wanders the eyes stray from center. As you bring the eyes back to center the mind follows. In sleep our minds are unconscious in meditation super conscious similar appearances opposite polarities.

It is interesting to notice that when the mind wanders the eyes stray from center. As we bring the eyes back to center, the mind follows. In sleep, REM (rapid eye movements) occurs when we are in a dream state. The eyes dart from side to side, accessing thoughts and memories. This same REM occurs in our waking mind and also in the early stages of meditation before the mind calms. That is why fixing the gaze on an external or internal object (heart or third eye) can be a great boon for meditators at any stage.

YOGIC DIET

It is best to choose a time of day for the practice when you feel fully awake and the stomach is light. The food we eat plays an important part in being able to sit comfortably and meditate.

Yoga being a complete spiritual path, has a formula for the best foods for spiritual practice, it is aptly called the *Yogic Diet*. It was formulated in ancient times so simple, clean, and easily digested foods could be chosen and consumed affording our bodies, minds and emotions a feeling of lightness and health. Try experimenting with eating a lighter diet using more fruits, vegetables, and grains and notice if it makes a difference in the quality of your practice.

If we look again to the three Gunas, all of nature, including food, reflects a predominance of one of three attributes.

When we choose foods in the *Sattvic,* or balanced Guna, they allow the natural vitality and health to be present in the body, as peace and joy are experienced in the mind. *Sattwic* food is simple and tasty, staying as close to its natural form as possible. When food is simple, we tend to eat less of it; our bodies are nurtured and satisfied, and our minds and emotions are in harmony.

Rajasic foods tend to be overstimulating and cause restlessness, disease, and agitation in the body, mind and emotions. It affects the peaceful qualities. Some food and drink, like meat and alcohol, at first have a stimulating effect and then cause lethargy. You might want to choose cautiously, if you are interested in having a deeper meditation practice.

Tamasic foods deplete—instead of enhancing—energy from body, mind and emotions. Food that is old or cold, overly fermented, moldy, or overcooked is considered *tamasic*. These foods can make you lethargic and unfocused. Dead and decaying foods *take* rather than give vitality and energy. The pot of soup you made last week stored in the back of the refrigerator probably has very little vitality left in it. Better to throw it away or compost it than to eat food that depletes energy. We need as much vitality and energy as possible for meditation, so be very frugal while choosing food in this *Guna*.

A MEDITATIVE EXPERIENCE

Eating with Consciousness

In the beginning of the practice, choose foods that have definite visual,
auditory, olfactory, and tactile sensations. After your senses are
cleansed, more subtle foods can be used.

Have the following foods cut on a plate before you.
a thick, fresh (not stale) cracker
a freshly cut wedge of lemon
a slice of a very ripe banana

After seeing the food, it is best to close the eyes
and let the other senses take over.

Pick up the cracker.
Feel its texture. Is it smooth or rough?
Using both hands, bring the cracker to your ear. Break it in two.
Notice how it sounds.
Bring it to your nose and notice if the aroma is stronger
where the cracker was broken.
Place it on your lips and feel its texture.

Take a small bite and allow it to dissolve
in your mouth without chewing.

Notice how it dissolves part by part.

Chew whatever is left and feel the sensation of swallowing solid food.

Can you feel it entering your stomach?
Sit quietly for a few moments and notice how you feel.
Next, pick up the lemon.
Feel its texture.

Does it feel wet? Cool?

How does the feel of the inner part compare with the rind?
Bring it up to your nose and smell the lemon.
Does just smelling it make you salivate?
Now bring it up to your lips and rub it on the inside of your lower lip.

Place it in your mouth and notice which part of the tongue
can taste the sourness of the lemon.
Feel the sensation of liquid moving down the throat as you swallow.
Can you feel it as it enters your stomach?
Sit quietly for a few moments and notice how you feel.
Next, pick up the banana.
Bring it up to your nose. How does it smell?
Squeeze the banana between your fingers.
What does it feel like? What is the texture?

Are you making an unpleasant face as you mash the banana
in your hand?

Smell it once again. Does it smell stronger than the first time?
Place a small amount in your mouth and notice
where the taste is recognized in your mouth.
Move it around with your tongue.
Can you make it dissolve without chewing it?
Notice the texture as it moves down your throat as you swallow.
Can you feel it as it enters your stomach?
Sit quietly for a few moments and notice how you feel.

Observe how each of the foods looked, felt, smelled, sounded, and tasted completely different, how each of your senses was engaged in a different way.

After doing this meditation, you will hopefully experience everyday food and eating with a new awareness. You can even do this in a modified form at mealtimes. You may notice that you eat less and enjoy it more!

Chapter Seven

Breath and Pranayama

a Prelude to Meditation

Prana - after asana
· Remove lactic acid
  before Meditation
· Redirect Prana from Ana
  to Vijana Kosha

From the Yoga Sutras of Patanjali

II. 49 The universal life force (*prana*) is enhanced through the harmonious rhythm of the breath (*pranayama*).

II. 50 The movement of the life force is influenced by inhalation, exhalation and sustained breath.

II-51 A balanced rhythmical pattern steadies the mind and emotions causing the breath to become motionless.

II-52 As a result, the veils over the inner light are lifted.

Goal of Prana

II-53 The vista of higher consciousness is revealed.

Continuing our preparation for Meditation, once we have steadied the body, we begin to enhance and guide the breath and vital life force (*prana*).

Pranayama's physical and mental effects have been touted through time. It is known for the extraordinary physical benefits it manifests in *healing* the body, mind and emotions. That aspect of Pranayama practice and the benefits it brings "while exemplary" will not be expounded upon here. For our purposes we will address the aspect of Pranayama that leads us into the stillness necessary for meditation. It is a wonderful practice allowing us to focus and dive deep within.

In breathing, we are satiated—not just with oxygen but with vital energy. We inhale precious energy called *prana, chi or qi*. This is the same life force we extract from food, light, and love. Although we take in *prana* in many ways, the breathing practices are the most effective way to channel that life force into all parts of the body, mind and emotions.

The *prana* secures our body's health through the proper digestion of food, warding off diseases and fostering an overall sense of well-being. The clearer and stronger the life force, essential to our survival, the better we look and feel. When our mind becomes clear, decisions are easier; the emotions find their right place and bring us renewed fulfillment in even the smallest things we do. Life can sail along at a smoother pace without so many bumps and valleys when this energy is *balanced*.

PRANAYAMA PRACTICES FOR MEDITATION
Deep Breath, Calm Mind

As babies, we belly breathe, developing our lower lungs first. Much of our early months is spent lying down. Our physical activity is minor compared to our rapid *inner* growth and development. There is a gentle, rhythmical in-and-out motion as the belly expands and contracts. This enables the lower part of the lung, which contains a higher concentration of alveoli (air sacs), to develop and receive much-needed oxygen. The next part to develop is the middle part of the chest and lungs. Then, as more of the activity is either sitting or standing, the upper lungs or apex develops.

Three Part Breath-Deergha Swasaam

Pranayama is a very important practice for physical energy and especially useful to calm the mind, emotions and senses before entering a state of meditation.

It is best to start with a simple aspect of *Pranayama*. By learning and practicing *Deergha Swasaam*, (three-part breath) we learn the basis of all breathing practices and create a strong foundation for the others to follow. By practicing deep three-part breath, we take in a greater quantity of oxygen that allows for more efficient distribution to the lower, mid, and upper (apex) lung. This gives us more available oxygen *and* more life force or *prana*. It then creates a specific physiological response that triggers the para-sympathetic nervous system to persuades the body to *relax* on each exhalation.

A MEDITATIVE EXPERIENCE

Three Part Breath

The first part of the three-part breath can be practiced while lying down in the relaxation position or sitting comfortably with the back erect.

Part One: Place your right hand so that the thumb rests at the naval and the fingers embrace the belly.

Inhale completely through the nose expand the belly, allowing the lower lungs to fill. As you exhale, contract the belly.

Inhale expand the belly; exhale, contract the belly. Continue until you feel comfortable with the practice.

Drawing of Part One

Part Two: Place your right hand on your belly and your left hand on the side of your lower ribs or on your lower chest.

Inhale and expand the abdomen and the rib cage; exhale and contract the rib cage and the abdomen; inhale and expand the abdomen and the rib cage.

Continue parts one and two of the three-part breath until you feel comfortable.

Drawing of Part Two

Part Three: For this next part, leave your right hand on the belly and place your left hand on your upper chest or collar bone.

Inhale expand the belly, the lower lungs, continuing to inhale to the upper chest. Feel the collarbones rise slightly.

On the exhalation, release the air from the upper chest, the lower chest, and the abdomen—one section flowing into the other.

Inhale and continue to expand the abdomen and lower chest, the middle chest and upper chest, so that the collarbones rise slightly.

Continue breathing slowly and deeply for a few minutes, and end with an exhalation.

Allow the breath to return to normal.

Sit quietly and find yourself being still and ready to enter meditation.

Drawing of Part Three

THE SUBTLE NERVOUS SYSTEM

There are thousands of subtle pathways or *nadis* within and
surrounding the physical body. The purpose of the *nadis* is to allow the
prana to circulate and distribute the much-needed energy to the
physical, mental and emotional bodies. The *nadis* distribute energy and
prana in a similar way to the blood vessels, carrying blood to all parts
of the body. Of the many thousands of *nadis*, three are most significant:
Ida, Pingala and *Shushumna*.

The *Pingala Nadi* and *Ida Nadi* polarize the neutral energy as they
wind around the spinal cord. As the prana circulates through the
Pingala Nadi, (the *HA* or sun qualities in *Hatha*) it generates heat and
the masculine attributes of rational thinking, intellectual and reasoning.
The *Pingala* also governs the *sympathetic nervous system* and
corresponds to the left side of the brain.

When prana circulates through the *Ida Nadi*, (the *THA* or moon in
Hatha), it produces a coolness and accesses the feminine attributes of
emotion, feeling, and intuition. *Ida* guides the *parasympathetic nervous
system* and corresponds with the right side of the brain.

The *Shushumna Nadi* only comes into play when the *Pingala* and *Ida*
are in perfect harmony. It then has the sacred duty to carry the *Prana*
through to the higher centers of consciousness *(chakras)* bestowing on
us spiritual realization. It *does not* function as the day-to-day distributor
of energy to the physical, mental or emotional bodies.

Sutle wants to go up

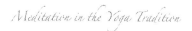

THE CHANGING PATTERNS

Having two nostrils supports the flow of energy through *Pingala* and *Ida*. Although most of us are probably unaware of it, the lining of each nostril engorges and shrinks periodically during the day. This shifts the flow of air from one nostril to the other in a biological rhythm. Everyone and a half to three hours the *Pingala* and the *Ida* alternate dominance, in hopes of restoring balance.

All of our physical systems depend on the regular flow of air *and* prana. If our habitual breathing patterns are upset or halted because of erratic movements in our body, the oxygen and energy requirements go up. If we suddenly run or quicken our pace, the breath accelerates, using up more *prana*. As we slow down, our breath follows.

If our bodies can change our breathing pattern, then the opposite is also true. A deep breath revitalizes us when we are tired. When we observe how these variations in breathing change our breathing according to our daily functions and moods, *pranayama* becomes an essential practice in returning us to balance.

Mental and emotional states also affect the breathing pattern and change nostril dominance. When we feel anger *or* passion, which are heating emotions, chances are our right nostril will be open. Depression *or* calmness may cause the left nostril to take over. At night, we turn from one side to the other dictated as the nostril dominance shifts.

Whichever side we are lying on, the opposite nostril is open. If you nap in the heat of day, the left nostril's vigilance allows you to rest deeply.

If, suddenly, the phone rings disturbing your sleep, the left nostril will engorge, causing the right nostril to release and allowing you to be present for the call. The body's consciousness is awake even when we are sleeping.

The mind and emotions host millions of thoughts and feelings that are perpetually hungry for energy in order to move about and function. These thoughts and feelings respond to the same rhythmical relationship the breath has with the body. With a long slow exhalation, they have room to spread out. The measured, rhythmical pace allows them time to consider whether and how they will manifest.

When a balance between the *Pingala* and the *Ida* is sustained over a period of time through various *pranayama* practices, the *prana* is then directed through the central *nadi*, the *Shushumna*. This centers the mind and emotions, moving them toward *Dharana* (contemplation) which leads to *Dhyana* (meditation) and ultimately to the highest consciousness *Samadhi*.

ALTERNATE NOSTRIL BREATHING PRACTICE-NADI SUDDHI

As the body becomes comfortable with the three-part breath, we are able to begin to regulate and balance the breath. Alternate nostril breathing is an exceptionally powerful technique for calming and relaxing the body, mind and emotions. A great prelude to meditation! This breathing practice is done in a comfortable seated position. For the purpose of learning to breathe deeply we practiced *Three Part Breath-Deergha Swasam* lying down. The position itself dissipates the energy, and that is not the effect we are looking for in most pranayama practice. If the concept is to focus and direct the energy upward a sitting position is optimal. We use the same three-part deep breath as we did before. The only difference is that we are breathing through only one nostril at a time.

REGULATING THE COUNT

Once ease and comfort come to the alternate nostril breathing, we can increase the balance between the nadis and nostrils, by regulating the amount of time it takes for the breath to flow in and out.

Ideally, we expect both nostrils to have the same capacity for intake and output. Usually that is not the case. Some like to count as a way to regulate the breath and many set the goal at a 2:1 ration-the exhalation being twice as long as the inhalation. With this process there is a tendency to cause strain trying to attain the goal and to expect that both nostrils are equal in capacity. Instead think of it as a prelude to meditation where ease and comfort are the appropriate aspects.

Count both the inhalation and exhalation of both nostrils and set the count based on the lesser of each. After noting the count from the right and left nostrils, choose the lower number and apply that to both. Do the same for the inhalation. For example, if the count from the right nostril is 5 and the left is 4, choose the count of 4 for both. Do the same for the exhalation. This will eliminate any cause for strain. As you feel comfortable the count can be increased equally in both nostrils and in small increments.

After a while, when you experience progress and ease in the practice, try letting go of the count, which is a left-brain function and enjoy the flow of breath.

For added enhancement try using a sacred word (mantra) or phrase. Measure the time it takes to repeat the sacred word or phrase and replace that with the number count.

Just by equalizing the breath you are balancing the sympathetic and parasympathetic nervous systems and the *Ida* and *Pingala*. This allows you to feel the peace and calmness balance brings, which then leads into a deep meditation.

HAND POSITION IN NADI SUDDHI

A MEDITATIVE EXPERIENCE

Balancing the Pingala (masculine) and the Ida (feminine) Through Alternate Nostril Breathing

This breathing practice is done in a comfortable seated position. It is a great practice to do anytime to calm yourself, or a wonderful gateway to meditation.

With the right hand make a gentle fist and release the thumb, the ring finger, and the little finger. This is a classical hand position from Yoga, called Vishnu Mudra (sustaining seal). If it is uncomfortable, you can use the thumb and index finger. The thumb gently presses the right nostril closed while the left nostril remains open. Then, the extended fingers gently close the left nostril and the thumb releases the right nostril. (The left hand is resting comfortably on the lap).

To begin, exhale fully through both nostrils. Close off the right nostril with your thumb and inhale slowly through the left nostril as you expand the belly and the lower lungs. Continue to inhale to the upper chest. Feel the collar bones rise slightly.

Close off the left nostril with the fingers and exhale through the right nostril, releasing the air from the upper chest, the lower chest, and the abdomen one section flowing into the other.

Inhale through the right nostril, expanding the abdomen and lower chest, the middle chest and the upper chest, so that the collarbones rise slightly.

Close off the right nostril with the thumb and exhale through the left nostril.

Continue this pattern. Exhale, inhale, switch nostrils; exhale, inhale, switch. Begin to practice for one minute and gradually increase up to three minutes or longer.

At the end of three minutes, as you come around to the right nostril, end with an exhalation. Allow the hand to come to the lap. Be still for a few moments with the eyes closed as you observe how calm and still the breath and mind have become.
Observe the relationship between the two.

HUMMING BEE BREATH-BHRAMARI

This is a fun, yet very effective, breathing practice for leading into contemplation and meditation. It is also, helpful for children or adults that have difficulty being still or drawing within.

This breath is the bridge between the inner and outer worlds drawing us inward to a state of meditation. The humming sound we produce invokes the *Pranava* – the cosmic sound of the universe. Hearing the subtle sound, we draw deep within to the cosmic vibration, leaving all external sounds. We are now invoking *Pratyahara*, withdrawal of the senses (discussed later in the book).

These humming sounds vibrate the skull, brain and the pituitary gland, which is located directly in the center of the head. This results in a toning effect on the master gland as it releases a plethora of hormones that promote a feeling of well-being. Try it before meditation and notice how easily you flow into stillness.

A MEDITATIVE EXPERIENCE

Bhramari Practice

Sitting with the spine erect, take in a deep three-part breath.

On the slow exhalation, keeping the mouth closed make an audible humming sound within the head—feel it on or behind the soft palate. Listen as you feel the vibration.

When the sound fades, inhale and repeat the sequence.

Repeat five times with different pitches—low, high, medium.

Observe where each pitch vibrates in your body.

After the fifth round, sit very still drawing further within. Enjoy the sense of stillness and the deep sense of peace.

Notice how easily you can now enter the state of meditation.

Chapter Eight

Pratyahara

The Senses Draw Inward

From the Yoga Sutras of Patanjali

ll-54 Encouraging the senses to draw inward is *Pratyahara*.

II-55 Glimpsing the inner light, the senses contently dwell within.

As we move toward meditation, our thoughts, emotions, and senses naturally draw within. This is called as *Pratyahara*. *Pratyahara* is the subtlest aspect of *Hatha Yoga*. It follows *Asana and Pranayama* on the journey to *Dharana-Contemplation*.

Most meditation techniques are actually *pratyahara* practices. Because the practices and understanding of *Pratyahara* are lesser known, the term *meditation* became popularized as it entices a greater number of people to delve into a deeper practice. *Pratyahara* techniques encourage the senses to draw inward, inspiring the mind and motions to follow. Thus, making *pratyahara* a prelude to meditation.

THE BEAUTY OF THE SUBTLE WORLDS DRAWS US INWARD

Gently cajoling the senses to draw within often starts with our strongest information-gatherer: the power of sight. More than seventy-five percent of information gathered from the external world is assembled from what we *see*.

Redirecting the seeing to an internal focus encourages all the other senses to follow. Because we load so many visual images in our minds, we continue to "see" even with the eyes closed. Often students learning to meditate are coached to establish their inward gaze between the eyebrows ("third eye") or at the heart center. With this slow and gentle training, the mind will gradually relinquish its projection of previously imprinted visual images.

As the "sight" firmly adheres to the inner world, the sense of hearing follows. Refining the level and quality of sound we regularly experience prepares us for the subtle internal sounds. The innermost melodies are orchestrated by the *prana* as it travels through the subtle nerve channels (*nadis*). We become captivated by a delicate hum or swish as it transforms into the celestial sound of bells, whispers and choirs of angels.

The external world will fail to amuse the senses as you visit an extraordinary world within. Entice the senses inward by envisioning a gentle light or flame, the sound of your heartbeat, the fragrance of roses, the sweetness of saliva, or a feeling of wellbeing. Find ways to see, hear, and feel beauty in the delicate world within. As the outward senses calm, meditation becomes effortless.

Beginning practice, we identify the senses as they reach outward. We notice we are distracted by a truck passing by, someone turning a light on, or the temperature changing. Often, we try to let the background noises be there without taking them in.

All of our senses have two components. As we draw further inward, we recognize the inner component of these senses. For example, our sense of hearing reaches out and reaches in. If you put your fingers in your

anahata Sounds = Sound of Prana moving through heart Chakra ears right now, you would eliminate outer sounds and you might hear your heart beating. If you gaze at a candle with your eyes open and then close your eyes, you see the candle flame manifested with the inner eye. Have you ever had a flashbulb go off in your eyes when a picture was taken of you? You walk around for a few minutes with red and yellow dots in front of your eyes. You see the dots with the eyes open or with the eyes closed, the outer and inner sight.

Begin by withdrawing the senses from the outer world. The more we draw the senses inward, the less we are distracted by externals. And the less we are distracted by externals, the quieter the mind and emotions get.

We then are conscious of our *inner* noises, thoughts shuttling back and forth in the mind. As we become still, we realize how much noise is created by the movement of the thoughts in our own mind. By continually drawing in of the senses, even the internal noises are quelled.

Many of us *choose* to be surrounded with background sounds. We have the television, radio, or headsets on all the time. It seems that we are trying to drown out the mind's noise by having louder noise outside — noise that we *can* control. It is difficult to experience true outer quiet in our modern society. Just take a moment now and notice if your home is quiet. Is the refrigerator humming? Is a neighbor playing music or starting a car? Even the soothing sound of a bird is outside noise. We must go inside to experience real quiet.

There was a study conducted at the University of California, Los Angeles, some years back that compared three of the major meditation traditions: Yoga, as a meditation tradition, Transcendental Meditation (TM, actually part of Yoga), and Zen Buddhism. Each group was asked to choose ten experienced meditators who had been practicing for at least five years (without a break and hopefully with a whole heart).

The researchers were trying to discern any differences between the three types of meditations when exposed to external stimulation. Were the meditators really able to draw within so as to not *hear* or *react* to any external noises? In other words, were the subjects in fact meditating?

TM (repetition of a mantra) and Yoga practitioners asserted when drawing inward, through *pratyahara* (withdrawal of the senses) the ears would no longer hear, and the body would stop reacting to external sounds. The Zen Buddhists claimed that they were ever present and would always hear and react. Let the meditations begin!

I arrived with some sense of wonder and excitement at the laboratory on my day of "testing." Blanket and pillow in hand, I was asked to sit and do my usual "meditation routine." However, before I began, my body was hooked up to an EEG, a device that measures brain waves. In meditation beta waves normally found in the active mind are replaced by calmer alpha waves and, with deeper practice, even theta waves. I was also wired to an EKG (measuring heart rate fluctuation) and a skin moisture sensitivity test. A set of headphones was placed on my ears and a video camera kept a vigilant eye on my every movement.

The researcher left me alone with the instruction to *meditate*. The laboratory theater was *not* the ideal place to practice meditation. The vibration was less than sublime. I transported my mind to a cave in the ancient Himalayas. Holding that image, I spent the next hour in *pranayama* (breathing practices) and meditation.

At an undetermined time, I began to hear little clicking noises at what seemed to be regular intervals. The regularity became irregular and more and more annoying. At a certain point they faded away.

At the end of an hour, the lights went on and I was released from my wire prison. A worried researcher asked if I was okay. "Yes, I feel great! Is there a problem?"

"At one point," the researcher told me, "your EKG and EEG slowed down to the point of concern. I almost came in and stopped the meditation. I observed you through the camera and you were still sitting upright, so I decided to leave you alone."

Smiling, I asked about the clicking. It seems that even though I thought I had heard the clicks throughout the entire period, my body and brain stopped reacting after the first few minutes. (Pratyahara-withdrawal of the sense of hearing). Even when I perceived the clicks erratic in time and duration, they were in fact evenly spaced and regular. This seemed to be the consensus with the other two disciplines as well. In fact, according to this study, there was no obvious difference between the three meditation techniques or the experiences of the meditators-once again proof that as quoted in an ancient scripture "Truth is one. Many are the paths."

Whenever choosing tools for our work or play, we must take the time to select the correct size, shape, texture, and level of use. I may like the look and feel of advanced skis: yet if I am a beginner, the skis specifically designed for that level suit me best. When selecting food for a special meal, we prefer food that is tasty as well as nutritious. It is with that same consciousness that we embrace a *pratyahara* practice.

Today there are many great techniques to choose from no matter how they are named. The goal of any technique is to keep the mind, emotions and senses engaged and focused until they become still. This is the role of *Pratyahara* as a preparation for Meditation.

A MEDITATIVE EXPERIENCE

Pratyahara - Drawing the Senses

and Awareness Inward

This is a profound relaxation practice for bringing in all of the outward sensual consciousness. We begin with the physical body, then move to the breath, thoughts and emotions.

Begin to take in a few deep breaths. Notice how still the body and breath become as they relax. Observe the breath without controlling it as it comes and goes without any strain.

Guide this gentle breath to bring all sensual awareness from the feet, ankles, lower legs, knees, thighs, hips.
Relax.

Guide this awareness to withdraw from the fingers, hands, wrists, forearms, elbows, upper arms.

Let go of holding awareness in the hands and arms, or shoulders.
Relax.

Do the same with the buttocks and pelvis, allow the abdomen to soften,
imagine the chest, lungs, the heart and the throat relaxed.
Gently allow the awareness from the base of the spine to slowly rise up
through the middle spine to the upper spine.

Relax the shoulders and allow the neck to be an open connection
between heart and head.

Experience the sensations as the body retreats.

The head holds most of the organs of senses. Gently relax the jaw and
withdraw taste and speech from the mouth.
Withdraw smell from the nose.
Allow the eyelids and the eyes to soften, moving toward the inner sight.

Relax the forehead and tune the ears to the inner sounds.

Relax the entire scalp and bathe the brain with relaxation. Relax.

Allow the gentle breath to relieve the mind
and emotions of all movement.
Relax.

Slowly bring the awareness to the gentle breath
as it enters and leaves the body.
As it enters, feel yourself drawing deeper within.

As it leaves, feel yourself letting go of all holdings.

Notice a lightness and a feeling of distancing from the body, mind, emotions and all worldly cares.

Begin to go further within to look for that place of stillness, peace and joy. This is the dwelling place of your Divine Self.

(Have five full minutes of quiet time.)

Slowly and gently bring the awareness back to the breath.

Begin to increase the inhalation and feel that the senses have been purified and strengthened. Begin to feel them awakening to a relaxed body, and a calm mind.

As you continue with this practice, your senses will become accustomed to drawing inward. It will become effortless to prepare the mind and emotions for deeper practice.

Chapter Nine

Meditation in Practice

We are very fortunate in these modern times to have many great practices that lead us into a state of meditation. The *best* practice is the one that *suits you best*, is uplifting, and you embrace it with a whole heart. Some practices may appeal to the more analytical, cognitive types (left side of the brain). Others appeal to more abstract, intuitive type (right side of the brain). There are some that appeal to both.

Choose for yourself, not just from popularity or convenience. There are many methods that are tried-and-true and have been used for thousands of years as they have a certain power associated with them, a buildup of energy. You may choose to take the superhighway (the tried-and-true) and later switch to a footpath (your own way).

After concluding your meditation send that peaceful energy out to the world wishing peace and joy to all. Use whatever words you would like; it could be an *official* prayer or an *unofficial* prayer from the heart. If you think of any people who are in need of good wishes, include them in your prayer as you hold them in your heart. After meditation we are open to all possibilities.

Continue to be still for a few minutes and allow the experience to seep in. The moments after meditation can be likened to the time directly after watering a plant. If the plant is moved too soon after watering, much of the water spills out. It does not have enough time to soak in. It seems to be the same with meditation. Allow the peace to go deep to water your soul.

GAZING - TRADAKA

Gazing, or *tradaka,* is an ideal practice that allows us to cross the bridge from *Pratyahara* to *Dharana (*meditation*)*. Withdrawing from the world of senses we are placed on the precipice of attaining stillness.

It is a useful practice for beginning meditation or for those days when the mind is overly active. This technique is one I have used when working with children. Tradaka starts with an external object and then draws us inward. The restless mind is allowed to observe something real, concrete. We use the outward and inward vision alternately; this keeps the eyes and the brain working together. Choose any outward object that draws you to it and inspires you.

A MEDITATIVE EXPERIENCE

Tradaka or Gazing

*This meditation is gazing. This is done with an external object. It could
be the delicate beauty of a flower or a simple candle flame, a
photograph or a geometric design. Anything that allows you to feel
quiet, peaceful. Place the object directly in front of you at eye level.*

*Allow the eyes to close and mentally observe the body make sure the
spine is erect, shoulders back and that you are relaxed.*

Take in a few deep breathes and let them out very slowly.

Allow the body to be still.

*When you feel that stillness slowly allow the eyes to open and begin to
gaze at the object you have chosen.*

Allow the eyes to remain focused and steady.

Observe the qualities of the object.

*As the eyes feel uncomfortable, tear or blink close them softly and
allow the image to appear in the mind's eye. As the internal image
fades open the eyes and again gaze at the object.*

Repeat this sequence several times.

Allow the eyes to close and follow the qualities of the object
as it goes deep within.

Slowly as you feel ready, begin to deepen the inhalation.

Allow the eyes to open slightly and see once again
the object you have been meditating upon.

Observe how you feel.

Slowly and gently bring the hands together and rub the palms,
generating heat. When you feel warmth from the hands, gently cup the
palms over the eyes. Allow the darkness and the warmth to penetrate
deep into the eyes and behind them, soothing away
any tension you might feel.

Very slowly bring the fingertips down and stroke the eyelids out toward
the ears, removing any tension or strain from the eyes.

Then return the hands to the lap.
Relax.
Observe how peaceful and centered you feel.

Shat Kriya

MEDITATING ON THE BREATH OF LIFE

Our breath is one of the miracles of life that we often are not aware of. Observe the breath and notice how it meshes the outer and inner worlds. As the waves gently come onto the shore and return to the sea, so our breath enters the body and then returns to the world.

The breath naturally flows in and out about sixteen times a minute, back and forth, in and out, gently and evenly. We often use the word *inspiration* to mean something that comes to us from a higher place. To inspire is also to breathe in. To expire is to leave the body, to let go and to exhale.

The rhythm of the breath is a wonderful and relaxing way to engage the mind. Many of us have sat for hours listening or watching the waves crashing on the shore. We now have the opportunity to observe the body's tide—the breath, which affirms life as it comes in and encourages us to let go and trust as it leaves. We can observe the coolness of the breath as it comes into the body and the warmth as it leaves. Experience the expansion and contraction of the belly, how the entire body seems to move in unison with the breath. We draw in from the world with the inhalation and on the exhalation, we return a little bit of warmth.

As we sit quietly observing the breath, we feel a oneness with the entire creation. We breathe the breath of every living thing. Rich or poor, good or bad, the breath comes in and out. You may find that judgment begins to fade and is replaced by an openness, an acceptance of the perfection of life's flow. Continue to focus on the rhythm of the breath which connects you with the rhythm of your own heart, the flow of the ocean of life. Being an ancient practice, it is also seen in the Buddhist tradition. A young student was asking a master what to expect after years of practice. He wanted to make sure it was *worth his while*.

"If I begin to observe my breath what will happen in two years?"

"You will watch your breath," replied the ancient priest.

"What if I watch my breath for ten years, what will happen?"

"You will watch your breath," was the reply.

"And after fifty years, then what?"

"Ahh!" said the priest, with a big smile. "After fifty years you and the breath will watch each other!"

LISTEN TO THE BREATH, SO-HUM

Once the practice of breath meditation is established, it can be enhanced by observing the sound of the breath. On its inward journey we can hear the sound, *SO* and on the outward journey *HUM*. As you observe the breath, engage the senses: feeling, hearing *and* listen. This can be done as a separate practice or combined with observing the breath. Tune in often during the day for a reminder of your true essence.

We now begin to observe the breath joining the outer world with the inner world. As the ocean gently comes into the shore and leaves again so our breath enters the body and then leaves. Back and forth in and out. Gently and evenly.

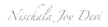

A MEDITATIVE EXPERIENCE

Listen to the Breath, So-Hum

Please observe the posture and when you feel ready allow the eyes to close. Take in a few deep inhalations and let them out very slowly.

Allow the breath to return to normal observe it as it slowly flows in and out of the nostrils easily without hesitation or strain. The breath of life.

Notice the difference in temperature. As the breath comes in it may feel slightly cool and as the air leaves it may feel slightly warm. The breath is the affirmation of life as we draw it into the body from the outer world and then we send our warmth back to the world.

Continue to observe the breath as it continues down into the lungs and causes the chest and abdomen to expand. As the air leaves feel the abdomen and chest release and relax. Continue to observe the natural flow of breath without force or control.

As you observe the breath -listen, can you hear a sound as the air comes into the nostrils? Listen closely to the sound as it leaves. Do they sound different? You may hear a slight hiss as the breath enters and a slight humming sound as it leaves. Listen to the sounds. Repeat them silently as the breath enters and leaves.

Observe the stillness of the breath. and observe the stillness of the mind and the relationship between the two. Slowly begin to increase the inhalation and as you feel ready allow the eyes to open.

THE WORD OR MANTRA

From the Yoga Sutras of Patanjali

I-27 Repeating the sacred sound manifests Divine Consciousness.

The word *mantra* has found its way into our common language usage today. It is always amusing for me to open the newspaper and find the word *mantra* in the comics or financial section. They are using it to mean a word that, when spoken, wields its own power. In the ancient Sanskrit language *Man* refers to "mind," *tra* "to transcend." A mantra is a word, sound, or phrase that, when repeated, allows us to transcend thoughts, mind, and our ordinary view of the world. The constant repetition of a mantra is called *japa*.

These inspiring words or sounds can come from many traditions, old and new. Those found in holy books or ancient languages have a certain uplifting vibrational quality. With these words, it is not *just* the meaning but a very special quality that has vibrated from the beginning of time.

In Christianity, the repetition of a word or prayer shows with devotional prayers to Lord Jesus, Our father and Mother Mary. Within that tradition prayers are "told" with prayer beads, or rosary. In the Russian Orthodox tradition, they are encouraged to repeat the Lord Jesus prayer continuously, in every waking hour. In Islam, sacred prayers are repeated five times each day, expressing great devotion. In

Judaism the blessings at mealtimes, sabbath, and sacred holidays are echoed from thousands of years to the present.

Words or prayers in ancient languages can be especially powerful when repeated with mind *and* heart. In Sanskrit *Om,* the universal consciousness, is chanted as the sound from which all other sounds resonate. *Shanthi* vibrates a feeling of peace. *Om Shanthi* then vibrates as the universal consciousness, peace. It is similar to the ancient Hebrew word, *Shalom,* which vibrates as a deep feeling of peace.

Notice how *Om Shanthi* and *Shalom,* are similar in sound and even in meaning. *Om, Amen,* and *Ameen* used at the culmination of prayer in *Hinduism, Christianity, Islam and Judaism* are words that seem to unite us in sound and *vibration* even if the traditions are diverse.

The idea of universal consciousness in sound may not always resonate to the nonbeliever. One nonbeliever I met, a nuclear physicist, was working on his neutron accelerator at a major university. I had the occasion to stay at his home when his wife, a Yoga teacher, invited me to give a talk at the university. After the evening event, the scientist and I exchanged dialogue. At first it seemed as if we were speaking very different languages, although we both spoke English. I was fascinated by advanced physics, even though I could not pass Physics 101!

He told me that a probe in the far reaches of the universe had just sent back a sound. This was a surprise to scientists at that time. Most expected the emptiness of space also to be void of any sound. The sound, when described to me, put a smile on my face. It was the cosmic hum or the *OM* sound!

Science and spirituality are only at opposite ends of the spectrum if it is linear. A circular pattern puts the two "ends" right next to each other! In the beginning, middle, and always is the sound or word.

If ancient words are not to your liking, choose more familiar words such as *one, peace, joy, love,* and the like, words that allow us to feel uplifted. Love goes all over the world. If you wish, put it in French *(amour)* or Italian *(amora)*. Choose a word, when repeated, whose feeling vibrates within you. Think how you feel when someone says the words, *I love you* and then say it to yourself—one hundred, two hundred times a day.

When we continually repeat *any* word or phrase, the cells in our bodies and our minds begin to vibrate with that sound. We take on the *qualities* of that word.

Can you think of the words you use every day? Do you have a pet word that may not be as sweet and as loving as it could be? Many of the little irritations of daily life may give you cause to use these particular words all too frequently: I missed that *blankety blank* phone call, or I didn't get that *blankety blank* parking space, or turning a block too soon and getting into a *blankety blank* traffic jam, missing the *blankety blank* bus, and on and on. Can you remember the last time you banged your toe on the coffee table? Did you say, *Om* or peace?

An example of a word that children often use is *yuck.* Suppose we began to use the word *yuck* each time we made a mistake: "Yuck this; yuck that." "Oh, that is yucky!" If you said it two or three hundred times a day, how would you feel by the end of the day? Very yucky!

In the same way, imagine saying *peace* two or three hundred times each day. That simple word would soon steady and uplift the mind and permeate your very being.

"How many times must I say this in order for you to understand what I am saying?" The answer is usually "Many!" Did you ever have to write a certain phrase on the blackboard over and over until you learned the lesson? Repetition in all forms allows us to change the way we think and feel.

There are many ways to repeat the word. When you are alone, repeat it aloud in a monotone or even a singsong or chanting fashion. In this both sides of the brain are engaged. The left repeats the word as language and the right enjoys the melody or tune. Say it softly, loudly, quickly, or slowly, depending on how the mind and emotions feel. Chanting in the original ancient language can still be heard on the holiest of days in each religion. It also seems to have modern significance.

Because of its remote location, a Catholic monastery on a small island off the coast of Italy, was able to keep many of its ancient traditions. In this particular monastery prayers were chanted in the Gregorian tradition as they had been done for countless centuries. Each new fledgling monk was carefully taught pronunciation and tone. Many hours a day were spent in chanting these sacred sounds and prayer.

When the new abbot was installed, he felt that too much time was being taken up in prayer and meditation. If the monks shortened the time in repetition of mantras, more productive work could be done.

After a few months, the monks started to fall ill. Some were unable to sleep, and productivity started to plummet. The water and food sources were examined. All were found to be pure. "What could be the problem?" the senior monks pondered. Physicians were called in from far and wide, with no avail.

As a last resort, an expert from America was summoned. He was researching the effects that energy from sound and chanting had on the physical body and mind. After a careful assessment was taken of the situation, he then gave his recommendations: Allow the monks to go back to their original scheduled hours of chanting and prayer. Their bodies and minds have been toned to a particular frequency, which allows them health and vitality. They will then be able to do more productive service in less time.

The chanting was restored and so was the health of the monks. It was later suggested by the research findings, that this type of chanting was so powerful even playing a recording in the background, while working, could elicit a calm and healing vibration. I am sure the same could be said for all of the chanting in ancient languages.

In workshops and classes, I often begin by asking everyone to chant *Om* together. At first, people are reluctant to chant, but after experiencing the uniting vibration, more join in. Chanting aloud has the benefit of repeating and listening to the mantra, almost simultaneously. Even if you feel you do not have a "good" voice, try chanting or singing a simple inspirational song softly to yourself. It will usually have such a calm and soothing effect that you will enjoy it often.

When you have become accustomed to the outward sound and vibration, permit the lips and tongue to repeat the word, delicately and thoughtfully, in a silent whisper.

Moving further in, let the mind repeat it in silence, the vibration touching the whole being as it vibrates as one sound. As all the cells align in the same direction, they are drawing the vibration of peace to you, like iron filings to a magnet.

With steady repetition of the mantra, the mind becomes very still so still that it does not even want to *repeat* the word. In this case the mantra may begin to repeat itself. This is called *ajapa,* "without repetition." Just let the effort drift away as you listen and enjoy the peace.

The next meditations allow us to experience two powerful aspects that combine to lead us to a deeper experience. The first being mantra meditation, meditation on a word or phrase. The second combines the breath with the word or mantra for meditation.

THE WORD OR MANTRA

For this meditation we use a word or phrase that makes us feel peaceful. These inspiring words come from different sources some from holy books, or ancient languages that have a certain uplifting vibrational quality. Words such as Amen, Ameen, Shalom, Om Shanti or more familiar words such as one, peace, joy, love, are all words that when repeated allow us to take on the qualities of that word. Imagine saying Peace 1, 2 or 3,000 times each day. That simple word would soon steady and uplift the mind permeate your very being,

A MEDITATIVE EXPERIENCE

Japa - The Word or Mantra

Choose a word or phrase that inspires you.

Allow the eyes to close. Please observe the posture. Slowly begin to observe the breath. Inhale and on the exhalation slowly and sweetly repeat aloud your chosen word. Continue the repetition with each exhalation. Peace, Peace, Peace.

Allow the verbal sound to become more and more quiet.

Allow the lips to repeat the word without any audible sound.

Allow the lips to be still and continue the repetition with the mind and heart.

You may combine the breath and the word. As the breath enters and leaves allow the mind and heart to silently repeat that special word. As the breath enters and leaves listen to the repetition of that special word.

Slowly and gently begin to deepen the inhalation - allow the eyes to open slightly -Be still for a moment and observe that feeling of deep dynamic stillness.

A MEDITATIVE EXPERIENCE

Breath and Mantra

This is a meditation on breath and word. Please have a comfortable seated position spine erect. Not leaning to one side or another forward or back. Close the eyes partially or fully.

Take in a few deep inhalations and let them out very slowly. Allow the breath to return to normal observe it as it slowly flows in and out of the nostrils easily without hesitation or strain. The breath of life.

Just as the ocean gently comes into the shore and leaves again so our breath enters the body and then leaves. Back and forth in and out. Gently and evenly.

Notice the difference in temperature. As the breath comes in it may feel slightly cool and as the air leaves it may feel slightly warm. The breath is the affirmation of life as we draw it into the body from the outer world and then we send our warmth back to the world.

Notice any outward sounds becoming further away as you draw inward.

Begin to silently repeat the special word you have chosen.

Combined with the in-breath. Hear the word whispered as the breath comes in. As the breath leaves allow the word to flow out as a wish to the world.

Keep the mind focused and allow the special word to draw you inward to embrace each part of the body and mind. --Leading you to Dynamic Stillness.

Slowly and gently begin to increase the inhalation.
Begin to softly repeat the word on the exhalation as a wish to the world.

Slowly and gently allow the eyes to open and behold the first rays of light. Continue to slowly open the eyes and allow the light from within to shine out into the world, wishing all peace and love.

SELF-INQUIRY

This meditation engages the mind to challenge the mind. With the same inquisitiveness that we use looking outward, we can look inward. When we observe a small child between the ages of two and four, this technique becomes clearer to us. Picking up a flower, the child might ask, "What is this?"

"That's a flower," we are happy to offer.

"What kind of flower?"

"A daisy."

"Where does the daisy come from?" And so, the questions continue until you have no answers for the child. Still the questions continue: "Why this color?" "Why is the sky blue?" Finally, it is the adult, not the child, who gives up.

In this form of meditation, the mind asks the mind questions or gives the thoughts in the mind labels: What kind of a thought is this? It is a *judging* thought? It is a *wanting* thought? It is an *observing* thought?

This practice allows us to be our own witness, we observe ourselves walking, eating, sitting, working. Each thought becomes a slow observation, not a mindless rush. Even our breath is labeled— "Breath in, breath out." It is the hope that the thinking mind will eventually give up.

I take this ancient meditation practice from the Jnana Yoga, or wisdom tradition. It could easily reflect a number of other wisdom traditions.

A MEDITATIVE EXPERIENCE

Who Am I?

Have the body in a comfortable position,
spine erect, shoulders relaxed.

Begin to observe the body. Check to see if everything is relaxed—the
toes, the feet, ankles, shins, calves, knees, thighs, hips, the hands,
wrists, forearms, and so on.

Through the nose, inhale and as you exhale, let that breath out very
slowly—and with it any tension that you might feel. Take in another
breath and let it out even more slowly. Feel yourself relaxing.

Place the sense of I in the center of the head.
Ask yourself:
Who am I?
Am I the body? The flesh? The bones? The blood? The organs?
No, I am not the body!

Who am I?
Am I the organs of motion?
Am I the arms that reach out?
No, I am not the arms or the action of reaching.

Who am I?

Am I the legs that propel the body to move and touch the earth?

No, I am not the legs or the movement of the legs.

Who am I?

Am I the organs of the senses?

Am I the eyes that see all sights?

No, I am not the eyes or the seeing.

Who am I?

Am I the ears that hear all sounds?

No, I am not the ears or the hearing.

Who am I?

Am I the nose that smells all scents?

No, I am not the nose or the smelling.

Who am I?

Am I the tongue that tastes and talks?

No, I am not the tongue or the sense of taste or the action of speech.

Who am I?

Am I the skin, the sense of feeling?

No, I am not the skin or the sense of touch.

Who am I?

Observe and experience your sense of:

the eyes and inner and outer seeing the ears and inner and outer
hearing the nose and inner and outer smells the tongue and inner and
outer tasting the tongue and inner and outer talking

Who am I?

Am I the mind?

No, I am not the mind.

How can I be the mind if I observe the mind?

I must be something other than the mind.

Who am I?

Am I the thoughts?

No, I am not the thoughts because I can observe and change the
thoughts.

Who am I?

Even the original I that was put in the center
of the head is not me because I put it there.

Who am I?

I am beyond all these things.

I am Absolute Truth, Absolute Knowledge, Absolute Bliss.

Who am I?

I am the one who knows.

HELPFUL ACCOMPANIMENTS
TO SITTING MEDITATION

WRITING MEDITATION-LIKHET JAPA

When sitting to meditate, if you find the mind is very agitated, *Likhet japa,* or writing of the mantra or word, can be just what is needed. Being placed on hold on the telephone can be very irritating, but mantra writing can be very productive for keeping the mind and emotions calm. Notice, to your delight, that when the person returns, instead of being annoyed for being kept waiting, you feel clear and ready to meet the next challenge.

In your preparation for Meditation keep a special notebook or a fresh piece of paper handy. If the mind is in need of calming, whether in the beginning or in the midst of practice, begin to form the letters of the word or mantra, you are using in silence. It is helpful to repeat them either silently or aloud *and* feel each sound vibration as it is written.

Write the word with intention and form each letter precisely. Let it create a perfect column or circle, so when it is observed from a distance it has a certain symmetry and calming feeling. Notice as the hand becomes occupied the mind quiets. This is especially effective if the word you have chosen does not have an everyday meaning for you.

If you are artistic, or up for some fun, draw an outline of a scene or design using the sacred word or words. If you do not have the talent to draw, use a coloring book, especially one that has mandalas. Adding the use of colored pencils or crayons to write the mantra and to fill in the different aspects can enhance the experience. Observe the balance of body, mind and emotions.

Always have a period of stillness at the end with the intension of drifting into silent meditation.

WALKING MEDITATION

Sometimes the body is not comfortable sitting for a long period of time. Instead of continuing to challenge it, walking can be done as an alternative to sitting meditation. It can be helpful to alternate sitting meditation with walking meditation until the body becomes comfortable sitting for longer periods of time. Sit for a prescribed amount of time, then walk, sit and repeat as many times as you choose. Make sure there is sufficient time for both aspects, rather than having any section too short to reap any real benefit.

It is helpful if you are doing this as a separate practice to begin with a moment of silence or even chanting OM, to establish that this is a meditation not just a gentle walk.

Clasp the hands behind your back as you begin to walk, taking slow, deliberate steps. Some prefer very slow while others go more quickly. The speed of the steps is completely up to your own rhythm. You may want to start faster and slow down as the mind settles.

Observe how and where you place your feet on the floor. Notice the entire body shifting its weight.

As the as the meditative walking is in progress, you can coordinate the movement of the body with that of the breath. For example, with each inhalation place the right foot on the floor. The exhalation comes as the left foot lands on the floor. If your steps are very slow, inhale as you raise the foot; exhale as the same foot is grounded.

As this process feels comfortable, a mantra or word can be added to the walking meditation. Each time you step with the right foot and inhale, silently repeat the word. Each time you step with the left foot and exhale repeat the word silently. In this way you are establishing a rhythm. When you observe that your step and breath have moved out of synchronicity, it means the mind has wandered.

After you have finished, be still either sitting or standing and feel the calmness. End as you would any meditation with sending love, light and peace to the world.

In walking, the body and mind stay united. The right and left sides of the brain function as one; neither is dominant. We are thinking and acting in balance. When we come back to sitting meditation, the balancing effect is dramatically felt. Some have told me they were unable to meditate until they tried walking meditation.

This is a wonderful adjunct to any sitting meditation. You can even use it walking from the car or bus on the way to and from work.

THE UNIVERSAL LIGHT WITHIN

There are times when it seems necessary for the intension of our meditation to move outward to sooth a difficult situation in our lives or in the larger world community. With all the distress and suffering people endure, we can develop our compassionate nature by sending love and light to a particular group or individual.

This meditation can be done at any time your heart wants to embrace others as yourself. It can also be done in a group for enhanced power.

A MEDITATIVE EXPERIENCE

The Universal Light Within

We will now have a meditation on the universal symbol-Light
Please have a comfortable seated position spine erect. Not leaning to
one side or another forward or back. Close the eyes partially or fully.

Take in a few deep inhalations and let them out very slowly.

Allow the breath to return to normal observe it as it slowly flows in and
out of the nostrils easily without hesitation or strain.

Slowly open the eyes and gaze at a candle flame
Begin to observe the breath
On the inhalation begin to draw that light into your heart. continue to
draw the light into the heart until you see one continuous light from the
candle to the heart.

As the light in the heart becomes brighter allow the eyes to close and
focus within.

Continue with each inhalation to see the flame in the heart brighten.

On the exhalation allow that same light to go out to the world as love.

On the inhalation the light brightens on the exhalation send the light
out to the world as love

allow it to grow and become the same size as the heart

to the whole body
beyond the body
to the room---the world

Slowly and gently begin to bring the awareness to the breath deepen
the inhalation -
Become aware of the light back in your own heart
Slowly allow the eyes to open just slightly - behold the first rays of light
coming in
continue to slowly open the eyes and allow the light from within to
shine out into the world. wishing peace and love.

Lokaa Samastaa Sukhino Bhavantu
Om Shanthi, Shanti, Shanti

May The Entire World Be Ever Blessed
With Peace and Joy, Love and Light.
OM Peace, Peace, Peace

Establishing a
Steady Practice

Congratulations on taking the giant leap toward knowing yourself. While reading *Meditation in the Yoga Tradition* the concept of forming a meditation practice is touted as a great beginning.

After going through and understanding the wisdom teachings and practices, now is the time to put into practice what you have read. Were there any times in the book that you thought, I really could use that? That really rings true for me! Perhaps, you even underlined something or wrote it down.

The difficult part of any great practice, especially meditation, is to do it. It is great to hear how everyone else can benefit, but will it really fit into your life? Will it work for you?

The best thing is to try it. From my experience the sooner you can begin practicing the quicker you will feel the benefits. Most of the benefits are subtle. You may not be aware of them at first. However, the advantage of enjoying a regular practice, the power is greatly enhanced. Dive right in while you are inspired. Be bold!

Another strategy is a little more conservative and for some it may be a bit more comfortable. Take one of the practices that seem most likely to bring benefit to you at this moment in your life. Practice it diligently for at least a month (less time is difficult to assess the effects). After a month begin to add another aspect of practice or increase the time in the practice you have already chosen.

Here are six good questions to ask yourself as you settle down to the practice. Write down the answers before beginning your practice. At first, you may want to review them on a daily basis. After some time, when you feel the benefits, the answers can be re-read for renewed inspiration.

1. Do I believe that a meditation practice is an important and key component to coping with stress, preventing disease and transforming my life?

2. What time of day will I do the practice? For how long? What will I use to inspire myself to practice regularly?

3. Which practices will I do, and will I combine a few?

4. Will the practice be done all in one time or divided into two or more sessions?

5. Where will I create a sacred space and what will it contain?

6. How will I incorporate the practices into my everyday life?

As you mold your future by inspiring yourself to go within and be still, you will find your life is infused with a sense of peace and a dynamic stillness to handle each new challenge with ease and integrity. More energy will then be available for that which is important to you and gives you joy.

You will then be able to honor your inner being as truth, light and love, beyond everyday thoughts and feelings. In those moments when you embrace that place in yourself, you are able to honor it in others. You will then radiate that joy to everyone you meet. Namaste

Om Shanthi, Shanthi, Shanthi

About the Author

NISCHALA JOY DEVI is a masterful teacher and healer. For many years she has been highly respected as an international advocate for her innovative way of expressing Yoga and its subtle uses for spiritual growth and complete healing. Her dynamic delivery and deep inner conviction empower each individual, allowing the teachings to expand beyond boundaries and limitations of any one tradition enabling her to touch people's hearts.

She was graced to spend many years as a monastic disciple with the world renowned, Yogiraj Sri Swami Satchidanandaji, receiving his direct guidance and teachings. She also was blessed with teachings from great Yoga masters in US, India and worldwide.

Originally trained in Western medicine, she began to blend western medicine with Yoga offered her expertise in developing the yoga portion of The Dean Ornish Program for Reversing Heart Disease and co-founded the award-winning Commonweal Cancer Help Program. Her book "The Healing Path of Yoga,".

With her knowledge of yoga and her experience in assisting those with life-threatening diseases, she created *Yoga of the Heart*, a training and certification program for Yoga teachers and health professionals designed to adapt Yoga practices to the special needs of that population. Passionate about the field of Yoga Therapy, a series of online classes were created to allow therapist to further their knowledge in different aspects of healing.

She is dedicated to bringing the Feminine back into spirituality and the scriptures, in her book, The Secret Power of Yoga, a woman's guide to the heart and spirit of the Yoga Sutras. and Secret Power of Yoga Audio book (Nautilus Book Award Winner). Understanding the need for more love and compassion in today's world, *The Namaste Effect*, her most recent book, explores a heart-centered way of living through the mystical chakras.

www.abundantwellbeing.com

Buddi - intellect   level
Manas senses   of
Amankara - ego Consciousness

Swami Visnu — Prana in
                  front

APP Asana/Prana/Pratyhara
  Hatha System
     Physical, energy, senses

DDS   Ontaro

108 - 1 - the singe Oneness of
      0 - everything & nothing all
      8 - ∞ infinity

mayru

Made in the USA
Middletown, DE
16 May 2021